Praise for Leaving a Charmed Life

In writing her stunning memoir, *Leaving a Charmed Life*, Kadian has fully stepped onto the path her soul intended and shows us all how to heal not only our current life but generations back—and forward.

 —**Ainslie MacLeod**, author of *The Instruction* and *The Old Soul's Guidebook*

Not all that glitters is gold. *Leaving a Charmed Life* is a must-read book that offers courage to face your own traumas and patterns. Kadian portrays how early childhood love, encouragement, and support can help to remedy what happened behind closed doors.

 —**Keith Shepherd**, Jamaican artist and dub poet

Kadian Grant's memoir is a touching and insightful account of her journey of self-discovery and survival. Through her raw and honest prose, Grant invites readers into her innermost thoughts and emotions, sharing a part of herself that is both vulnerable and empowering. Her memoir is a testament to the power of self-discovery and exploration and is sure to captivate readers with its heartfelt and relatable story.

 —Suzie Housley, **Midwest Book Review**

Kadian Grant bravely bares all as she details her inner journey towards forgiveness and endeavors to break patterns of abuse that span generations. *Leaving a Charmed Life* begs the question: what would you be willing to risk to pursue your own happiness?

—**Christine Herbert**, author of *The Color of the Elephant*

Kadian Grant has a way with words. While we expect that from an author, this is extremely impressive in a freshman effort where her soul is so very open. [...] This is a quick read. This is a deep read. It is not an easy read, but a s'hero's quest should not be. The darkness is real. The work Ms. Grant does is real and the battle we know is uphill and ongoing. When the goal is achieving authentic happiness, is that effort possible? Spoiler alert—the answer is YES! The "why" you know. The "how", you need to know. [...] Fellow warriors, those of us who have battled some of the same demons, or have those they love who may be locked in that battle now, will have a great opportunity to give a gift of importance.

—**Sherri Rase**, reviewer for *Out in Jersey* magazine and [Q]onStage

leaving a
CHARMED
LIFE

leaving a CHARMED LIFE

A TRUE STORY OF CHOOSING AUTHENTIC HAPPINESS

KADIAN GRANT

CREATIVE
COURAGE
PRESS

Creative Courage Press (Palisade, CO) www.CreativeCouragePress.com
(970) 812-3224 | hello@creativecouragepress.com

Excerpt from *Messages from the Masters* by Brian Weiss. Copyright 2000. Used by permission of Brian Weiss.

Library of Congress Cataloging-in-Publication Data

Names: Grant, Kadian, author. Title: Leaving a charmed life : a true story of choosing authentic happiness / Kadian Grant. Description: Palisade, CO: Creative Courage Press, 2023.

Identifiers: LCCN: 2023909211 | ISBN: 978-1-95992-100-4 (paperback) | 978-1-95992-101-1 (ebook)

Subjects: LCSH Grant, Kadian. | Adult children of dysfunctional families--Biography. | Mothers and daughters--Biography. | Child abuse--Bronx (New York, N.Y.)--Biography. | African Americans--Bronx (New York, N.Y.)--Biography. | BISAC BIOGRAPHY & AUTOBIOGRAPHY / Personal Memoirs | BIOGRAPHY & AUTOBIOGRAPHY / Cultural, Ethnic & Regional / African American & Black | BODY, MIND & SPIRIT / Inspiration & Personal Growth

Classification: LCC RC455.4.F3 G73 3023 | DDC 616.89/092--dc23

First edition (all formats): 2023

This work depicts actual events in the life of the author as truthfully as recollection permits. While all persons within are actual individuals, some names have been changed to respect their privacy.

Cover design: Karen Polaski

Cover photo of author as a child: Morais Studio, Jamaica

Ackee photo: Anthony Simpson. Ackee art: Keith Shepherd and Claude Pierre-Val

Editor: Shelly Francis. Editing Intern: Annalyse Hambleton.
Proofreader: Rebecca Job

To my three beautiful children, Kamilah, Khaleel, and Kyra. You are my greatest inspiration. I am in love with all of you.

Mama, my first embodied horizon, I love you.

Contents

1. Remembering Authentic Happiness   1
2. Love Was My Beginning   5
3. I Wish I Didn't Live Here   19
4. Get Out!   31
5. Landing in Depression's Cold, Dark Room   47
6. Escaping Depression's Cold, Dark Room   65
7. Unhealthy Unloading   83
8. Generational Patterns and Family Secrets   97
9. An Inspiring Year   113
10. A Guided Visitation to Remember the Past   131
11. The Year of Honesty   147
12. The Year of Nurturing   167
13. Leaving a Legacy   183
14. Rewriting My Story   189

Acknowledgments   193
About the Author   195
About Creative Courage Press   197

CHAPTER ONE

Remembering Authentic Happiness

I remember sensing something greater than myself as a four-year-old living in Jamaica. It happened on one of our family outings to the beach, my favorite activity as a child. We only went about three times a year and my excitement always kept me up the night before.

Even though I lived in the impoverished neighborhood of Waterhouse, my step-grandfather, whom we called Papa, owned an automobile. He had a 1961 Austin Cambridge that he painted blue from its original gray color. We were the only family in the neighborhood with a car in the sixties and early seventies. Papa on occasion was like the neighborhood's Uber driver, except he didn't charge anyone. He drove many families to the hospital or clinic for the arrival of their newborn or if someone fell ill or to help in any way possible.

His Austin Cambridge seated five passengers comfortably, but our outings consisted of my grandparents, two uncles, an aunt, my twin brothers, and myself. With so many people going, my brothers and I had to sit on someone's lap since we were the youngest. Most often, I had to sit in the rear middle spot because Adrian and Brian had to be apart from each other or else they'd fight the whole journey.

Grandma did not go on this trip, so my older uncle sat in the front passenger seat, and I got to sit on his lap. I rolled the window down all by myself, feeling grown up doing so. When we drove through the gate, the dogs bolted after the Austin, wanting so desperately to come on our outing. Adrian and Brian spun around and cheered on the dogs, "Come on!" and "Run, run, run." I laughed aloud, observing the drama from the left side mirror (Jamaica is a right-hand drive country). The dogs followed until they were tired, then we waved goodbye to them, and Adrian and Brian faced forward once again.

On the way, Papa stopped by the roadside vendors to buy mangoes, guinep, and coconut water to "wash off our hearts" (a Jamaican saying indicating one of the many health benefits of the coconut). We all piled out of the car to snack and socialize. After our bellies were full, I crawled back onto my uncle's lap, and we were on our way. We soon came upon the familiar forest of trees that would guide us to Hellshire Beach. I loved watching their gigantic leaves sway back and forth at the hand of the wind. I perked up at the sudden flash of turquoise that jutted from beyond the branches. Then, more flashes of turquoise appeared, and it seemed a game of peek-a-boo was on its way. I took delight in the ambient sound of the wind, its own unique tone carried by the ruffled leaves.

Wisps of the salted sea teased my nostrils, and I inhaled its freshness. I could hardly contain myself when the crisp, cool breeze separated the branches and unveiled the limpid blue sea. And it seemed our game had ended. The breeze caressed my face, scattered my plaits, and massaged my scalp. I was becoming drowsy, so I put my left arm on the door of the car to catch my falling head. I took slow deep breaths, falling in and out of consciousness, and melted in the serenity.

I stuck my hand out of the window, opening and closing my fingers, pretending to squeeze the breeze, then release it. Moments later, all molecular structure around me vanished, and I floated in its fluid space. I smiled from ear to ear, enjoying this experience, until my uncle's tactile tickle jerked me back to our present time, and I landed back on his lap.

"Why are you smiling?" he asked.

I giggled and said, "'Cause I'm happy!"

That unfamiliar presence stayed with me as we approached Hellshire. When we arrived, I ran onto the beach, still smiling because this presence continued vibrating within me and around me. I spun around until I fell onto the white sand. A light so bright demanded my attention, and I gazed upon its vastness. Beyond the glistening water, I saw a horizon with an uncontested beauty that froze me. I felt enticed and entranced. I gave in to the horizon's allurement and somehow knew my life was also limitless. At four years old, I felt that a greater purpose than Waterhouse, Jamaica, awaited me.

I stood up and looked around. Everything seemed anointed with a blinding luster. The sand, seawater, fish, rocks, all of it imbued with the horizon's beauty. I twirled as fast as I could, hoping to disappear into its bigness and traverse the continuum, when I heard "Charm, Charm, Charm" in the distance. The calling of my name jolted me out of blissfulness and steadied me in the sand. I saw my twin brothers running towards me with a gleeful-ness that expanded my heart. They were having their own bliss, but I knew it was only a modicum of what I had felt.

This day at the beach left an indelible imprint on my human consciousness and a yearning for authentic happiness for decades to come. I never had that experience again in Papa's car. After that day, I cried whenever I couldn't sit by the window going to the beach. No one knew the real reason why I cried because I couldn't put words to the experience for them to understand. My family thought I was just behaving like a spoiled child. But I had shared in something grand, and the life that had beckoned me on that day was now antagonizing me. I thought it was the magic of sitting by the open window that brought it forth.

On my journey as an adult to reclaim my authentic happiness, I recalled this soul-opening moment. If I had retrieved it more often from childhood to adolescence, I might not have settled so easily for external happiness or a small existence. This beach-breeze memory waned over time. It was not long before I re-tuned to my existing reality. But throughout my life, I had special people as embodied horizons who stood in its place as reminders. They planted seeds within me of who I really was and would assist in correcting my course if I were thrown off.

CHAPTER TWO

Love Was My Beginning

M y life story began with me jumping into Ms. Brown's birth canal in 1966 when she was seventeen years old and concealing myself in her womb. Ms. Brown was disappointed about being pregnant because my father was already residing in the United States, and she was afraid he wouldn't own the pregnancy. Also, she was in her last year of high school and wanted to graduate then go on to nursing school. That was the future she wanted for herself.

She was still having her menstrual cycle, but Grandma took Ms. Brown to the doctor when she saw her breasts growing. The doctor confirmed my mother was with child. Grandma wanted Ms. Brown to have an abortion because she was unsure of my father's involvement since he was no longer in the country. Even though Ms. Brown wasn't ready to be a mother, she did not want to terminate the pregnancy. When Grandma took her back to the doctor to inquire about an abortion, it was too late. Her test results showed she was already four months along.

Ms. Brown finally mustered up enough courage to go to the telephone company to relay the news to my father. He agreed that he was the father but wanted to know why she waited so long to tell him. She explained that her cycle hadn't stopped, therefore it hadn't crossed her mind. She also conveyed her mother's concern about the baby's financial future. My father told my mother to ask Grandma to call him.

Grandma and my father had a lengthy talk, and he assured her of his duty as a father. The conversation seemed to calm Grandma as she was no longer quarrelsome about the situation. Ms. Brown had to give up the future she envisioned for herself to stay home. A pregnant girl was not allowed to continue on in school in Jamaica.

In the early stage of Ms. Brown's third trimester, my father came through on the promise he made to Grandma on the phone. He shipped a crib, pram, baby formula, lots of clothes, toys, and everything he thought I would need. No one had ever seen a crib like the one my father sent, and I was the first child to have a pram in the neighborhood. Ms. Brown once told me, "Everyone envied you, and you weren't even born yet." My father provided for my birth and all of Ms. Brown's needs. He sent lots of pretty dresses when he heard he had a daughter. Grandma felt more secure about my financial future and trusted that my father would stick around.

Ms. Brown slept in Mama's bed closest to the wall her entire pregnancy. Mama was my great-grandmother. Ms. Brown lived with her for most of her childhood into adolescence. Ms. Brown would say, "Mama meant the world to me. She was more of a mother to me because I spent more time with her than my own. She was always there for me." Unlike Grandma, Mama wasn't upset about Ms. Brown's situation. She viewed it as something that had already happened, and everyone just needed to accept it. Ms. Brown said Mama was immediately overprotective. "She didn't want me to leave the house. She monitored my eating. She spoke to you constantly." Mama's love for me went beyond the grandparent syndrome of over-loving the grandchildren. I was hers before I was born.

One night, in January 1967, Ms. Brown opened her eyes to see something large and black on the ceiling. When the bat flinched, she screamed and jumped over Mama to escape, but Ms. Brown's foot got caught in the sheet, and she landed hard on her belly. She was overcome by her fear of flying animals and hadn't noticed the terrible pain she was in or the water trickling down her leg. Unable to stand and breathing heavily, Ms. Brown crawled to the next room on her hands and knees and sat behind the curtain that separated the rooms.

Mama rushed past Ms. Brown into the kitchen, grabbed the broom, and re-entered the bedroom, like a boxer entering the ring of a prize fight. Ms. Brown said, "I knew that bat wasn't going to survive when I saw the determination on Mama's face to get it away from her unborn grandchild." The curtain closing was the boxing bell ringing, and Mama and the bat entered the fray. Mama was immediately on the attack and the bat on the defense. Every time Mama swung, the bat dodged the broom, flitted around her head, and pitched on an adjacent wall. In desperation, Mama flung the broom in the bat's direction and missed. "You better get out of here," she warned. Mama picked up the broom and swung again but missed once more. "You're not welcome here!" She missed again and again, and it seemed the bat was just toying with her.

Mama went from trying to time the bat's landing to swinging in a frenzy. With every swing she yelled a different word, "You're... not... staying... in... here... with... my... great... gran..." Then the bat took a hit and landed on the bed. "You little wretch," shouted Mama in victory, but the bat swiftly recovered and pitched onto the wall. Mama's determination to protect unborn-me outmatched the bat's stamina.

This tussling went on for about fifteen minutes. Finally, Mama swung as hard as she could, and with what seemed like her last breath, struck the bat, and it fell on the tiled floor. Standing over the bat was a woman who would protect me at all costs. Mama quickly placed the broom on top of it, and yelled out to Ms. Brown, but she didn't respond.

Mama exited the room and glanced down at my mother sitting in a pool of clear water. "Are you all right?" she asked, panting.

Ms. Brown followed Mama's eyes to her crotch and sobbed with embarrassment, "I peed on myself."

After assessing the situation, Mama said, "That's not pee, your water broke." Mama watched her vigilantly and prayed through the night until it was time to go to the hospital.

I obviously survived the bat saga and entered this world the following night, unharmed, in my birth land of Kingston, Jamaica. When Ms. Brown returned from the hospital, Mama whisked me away from her arms and took me into the house. She didn't want anyone's "jealous" eyes on me. She didn't want anyone to touch me. It would be months before she allowed anyone to take me out of the yard. Mama's protection of me never waned.

My godmother, Aunt Steph, named me Kadian. She traveled often and was out of the country for my grand entrance. But when Aunt Steph returned home from her travels, she gifted me with a book and kept calling me her *lucky charm*. She visited me often and would shout from the gate, "Where is my charm?" Or if someone was holding me, she'd say "Give me my lucky charm!"

Everyone started calling me Charm after that. Kadian was now one aspect of who I was, but nonetheless, the greater aspect. And my family used Aunt Steph's doting words to create Charm, my other aspect.

Ms. Brown left abruptly for the United States when I was five and a half months old. I remained in the care of her side of the family, living with Mama, my grandparents, and their three children. Mama became my full-time caregiver, while Grandma tended to her bar and grill business six days a week. This home was dysfunctional, chaotic, and often violent.

A few months after Ms. Brown arrived in America, she was with child again. My parents decided it would be best if she gave birth in Jamaica, then rejoined my father to continue building the life they wanted for all of us. It would've been difficult to do that with a newborn. Ms. Brown returned to Jamaica during her third trimester, where the doctors informed her that she was having twins. My brothers, Adrian and Brian, were born in November 1968. When my father visited three months later, my parents were married, and he stayed awhile to spend time with us and his other four children from a previous marriage. My mother returned abroad when Adrian and Brian were about six months old.

My father continued providing financial assistance to Grandma. He also sent money monthly to finish the construction on her home. It was one of the better homes in our area after completion. Every year my parents shipped barrels filled with necessities like food and clothing, plus other things. I had jewelry, loads of dresses with matching shoes, and toys. I even had a doll that crawled when you pushed a certain button.

In the evenings, my family would bathe me, put me in one of my fancy dresses, and place me on the verandah like I was on display. People used to say that I looked like a doll. I wasn't allowed to run around barefooted like everyone else. Our neighbors weren't allowed to play with me and my brothers or to touch us. My cousin once said to me, "Even though we lived in the same house, I was poor, but you weren't. I was treated like the help, and you were treated like a prized doll."

My brothers and I were left in Mama's care during the day while my grandparents, uncles, and aunt were gone. Mama was everything to me and one of my early embodied horizons. Mama had an irresistible smile and an infectious laugh. She was committed to her religion and quoted biblical scriptures often. She wore long dresses only, spoke softly, and never swore. Her role in my life was indispensable.

Every morning Mama smudged the house of all bad energies with prayers. She made us get on our knees to give thanks to God for our rising, then she prayed hard and long. She told us how powerful God was and that He can change our situation instantly. All we had to do was ask.

After prayer, my brothers and I were given a teaspoon of cod liver oil, followed by breakfast. Sometimes, Mama prepared two or three separate dishes because we each wanted something different to eat. I always wanted rice porridge, and my brothers wanted corn meal. After breakfast, our world became magical. Mama watched us from her favorite chair in the back of the house while we climbed the trees in the yard, chased the chicks and chickens, laid our heads on the dogs in the sun, and ate from the fruit trees, whatever was in season—mango, guinep, cherry, sweetsop— except the ackee tree. We wouldn't eat straight from the ackee tree because *that* fruit needed careful preparation.

We had ackee and saltfish often during ackee season. Mama only picked ackee pods that had already opened naturally because if they are forced open, the hypoglycin levels are too high, and eating them will be fatal. I was taught that this toxin gets released upon the ripe ackee opening itself, which is the indicator for safe consumption. Even if the ackee pod only opens a little, that's enough to release the poison. A pod consists of three fruits inside, but on rare occasions, a pod will surprise you with four fruits.

My brothers and I often fought for Mama's attention. Adrian and Brian competed in soccer on the verandah, while Mama cheered them on. I sat between her legs and read my books to her. Mama never dressed me up. She let me wear shorts and sneakers.

Mama was always on edge when my aunt and uncles returned home in the evening. Our idyllic manifestation temporarily vanished along with Mama's smile as an uncharming world imposed itself between us until dawn rose again—a dysfunctional reality that functioned on bickering and violence.

My brothers and I lived amongst beings who did not revere the lives of humans or animals, and we saw this through the violence that occurred. For instance, my older uncle's rage on the family was perplexing. He would beat on his younger brother and sister, chase them with a machete, or kick them like a soccer ball. If my grandparents were home and they tried to intervene, he would beat on them too. My uncle didn't hit me or my brothers because he feared my father. He knew my father had friends who kept a watchful eye and would let him know if anything was happening to us, and it would only take a phone call to end it all.

Mama hated for us to witness the daily violence so she would usher us to the back of the house, sit on her favorite chair, and hide us underneath her long frock to protect us. To drown out the profanity and other terrible things that were said, she would sing her favorite hymn, "Blessed Assurance," and belt out the chorus "This is my story, this is my song." Then she'd whisper to us, "Jesus will always protect you." It seems Mama was trying to convey that this would not be our life.

Along with the violence, the occupants of the house weren't very educated—therefore they did not honor education or envision bigger lives for themselves. I could tell because they blended into their environment well. There weren't talks of being anywhere else even though they had family abroad. They bought into their small existence. They had lost familiarity with their horizon. Mama knew living in Waterhouse with my family was a meager existence and she did not want that for me. She unknowingly worked every day for me to not forget my horizon. One example was to empower me through books.

Every day I had to read out loud while she combed my hair. When I couldn't pronounce a word, she'd tell me to sound it out instead of telling me. Which was frustrating because I couldn't understand why she wouldn't just say it. I found out later that Mama couldn't read.

I loved books because of Aunt Steph. She always brought me one or two when she returned from her travels. I loved how they felt, and I loved to look at the words on the pages. She brought books I couldn't read yet, but insisted that I learn. She would read to me and teach me new words whenever she visited. One Christmas, she took me to downtown Kingston to buy my Christmas gift. I remember getting on an escalator to a tiny bookstore on the top floor. She let me pick any book I wanted. Aunt Steph never bought me toys, jewelry, or clothing.

Aunt Steph was another one of my early embodied horizons.

She not only named the greater aspect of me, she tried to help Kadian remain dominant by planting stories of other places and experiences within. They were seeds of a greater existence to germinate on my earthly journey that would whisper to me when I needed to be reminded of who I really was at the core. She too understood that my life was bigger than where I landed.

Mama also empowered me with love and support. She often told me how smart I was. When I wrote a letter to my parents at four years old, Mama took me on the bus across town to the post office. I don't recall much about the trip, but I remember how I felt when Mama picked me up to hand my letter to the letter carrier with my not-so-straight handwriting on the envelope. The letter carrier asked if I wrote the letter myself, and I nodded yes. When I turned and looked at Mama, I saw how proud she was of me. I was her world, and she was mine.

Most of my family members I lived with in Jamaica were not embodied horizons for me, except Mama and Aunt Steph. My early childhood in Jamaica mostly had a negative effect, even though Mama tried her best to shield me from witnessing the many violent indiscretions. An aggression was growing inside of me and sometimes erupted in my own angry outbursts. Mama couldn't contain the change from happening, for I couldn't un-see or drown out what I heard in that home.

After that beach-breeze memory, I began sensing a duality that existed within me, my greater aspect nudging me out of the slumber I was beginning to yield to. A reminder to turn away from a life that was not destined to be mine. Reminding me that I wasn't Charm. Mama's teachings were in line with my greater aspect. Mama spoiled me but also disciplined me. Sometimes with a glance or stare, at times with her proffered wisdom. I could tell she didn't want me to lose who I was at the core.

When I was about five years old, my brothers found a book of matches. They took turns trying to strike a match. After several missed tries, Brian handed it to me and told me to do it. This felt wrong immediately. I did not want to do what my brothers asked, but I took the book of matches anyway.

I stood there for a few seconds, for a higher consciousness with a message of greater capacity seemed to want to reveal itself to me. Striking the match was in opposition to who I was. A more powerful, not-so-connected me seemed in control. Those moments most often occur in seconds, and it can be difficult to choose your authentic self in a split second unless you are practiced at noticing. My five-year-old self was not practiced at noticing!

Then I heard Adrian say, "Do it, Charm! Do it now!"

Adrian's shouting brought me back to the present time. Without thinking, I struck the match and threw it on the bed. The match burned through the bedspread, then the sheets, and when I saw the mattress on fire, I grabbed my brothers and ran to Mama, who was in the back of the yard picking the open ackee pods to prepare for our lunch.

"Fire, fire!" yelled my brothers. "Come quick, Mama! Fire! Fire!" I don't recall saying anything. I remember being frightened by what I had just done.

Mama entered through the back door and screamed upon seeing the room aflame. She ran next door for help. People in our community didn't have landlines in their homes so they couldn't call the fire brigade. Your firefighters were your neighbors. One neighbor screwed a hose to the outdoor pipe and sped toward the room's window. Another neighbor filled buckets with water and passed each one to the other helpers to douse the mattress and curtains from the room's entrance.

Mama sat us down on the front verandah and asked angrily, "Who did this?"

Adrian and Brian both pointed at me, saying, "Charm."

I hugged my knees and cried.

Adrian and Brian were enjoying the excitement. They kept wanting to go inside the house to see what was happening. Two women neighbors picked them up and held them tightly at their hips to prevent the boys from getting in the way. I cried every time Mama looked at me with disappointment and shook her head. I felt ashamed. The neighbors saved the day. No one was hurt, and the news traveled to my grandmother's bar and grill. When I saw Papa's car coming towards the house and my grandmother with him, I knew I was in big trouble.

I got a whooping from Grandma and was sent to bed early. Adrian and Brian were not punished. Everyone felt I should have been responsible enough not to listen to them. My parents had to send money to replace everything in the room.

That night Mama asked, "Charm, why did you do it?"

"Adrian and Brian told me to, Mama," I said with remorse.

"Did it feel right to you?"

"No, Mama." I looked down at my feet, feeling ashamed. What my grandmother said next stuck with me.

"When something doesn't feel right to you, don't do it!" She looked at me sternly, disappointed with my choice.

I understood exactly what she meant. I had noticed a greater awareness before striking the match, yet I chose to listen to my brothers. That decision almost burned the room down. I got into trouble and made Mama disappointed in me. I didn't always adhere to her words growing up, but I remembered them.

My brothers and I were a pod on Mama's own ackee tree, a family tree that consisted mostly of forcibly opened pods that were poisonous to their environment. She tried to keep us in our pod to preserve our innocence, give us a sense of safety, and not expose us to the world too soon. Or else we would become individuals contributing unmindfully to this world, and our life's journey could deem fatal to our well-being.

Soon after the fire, my parents visited us. There was great excitement in the house. When they arrived, my brothers darted towards the rental car with open arms to greet them, but I stayed with Mama, hanging onto her thighs. She tried to nudge me forward, but I wouldn't budge. My family had shown us pictures of Ms. Brown, saying, "This is Fay. This is your mother." I knew who she was. I just wasn't sure about the mother part.

My parents picked up Adrian and Brian, kissed them, and swung them around. But I still couldn't move. I saw the disappointment on my mother's face when I didn't do the same. Neither she nor my father tried to coax me from Mama's side. They just left me where I was. My brothers called them "Mommy" and "Daddy," but I didn't call them anything. They felt like strangers to me. I didn't know how to feel about them. I remained very quiet during their visit.

My mother brought more dresses, shoes, and pretty barrettes for me. I hated them. She even brought me a red perfume bottle identical to the one she had. I didn't like the smell. It was too strong and made me sneeze. I still don't wear perfume because it irritates my senses. She hated that I ran around, climbed trees, and got dirty with my brothers. Every day my family styled my hair and now dressed me up twice a day to please Ms. Brown. I wasn't allowed to run around with Adrian and Brian, so I sat on the verandah with Mama. Ms. Brown said I should act like a little girl. I could tell she wanted a prissy daughter, but I was a tomboy.

My parents focused most of their attention on Adrian and Brian. My father was impressed and in awe of his twin sons, and my mother was disappointed in her only daughter. I think Mama noticed because she gave me more attention than usual. She knew I was feeling left out. My parents took us to the beach more than once and on other fun-filled outings. I warmed up a little towards them during their brief visit but still stood close to Mama.

When my grandparents took me and my brothers to the airport to see my parents off, my brothers and I cried uncontrollably. Even though I didn't feel close to my parents, it had been special having them around. Their presence made the house feel unified. The violence occurred significantly less because everyone was on their best behavior due to my father. Also, my father took us everywhere with him, and it felt like we were a real family. Our sadness at their departure lingered long after they left.

As last words of comfort, my father said to us, "You'll be coming to the United States soon."

Grandma locked away my perfume bottle, and no one cared about my hair or dressed me up twice a day anymore. I ran around with Adrian and Brian as usual. My days were magical again.

A year later, in October 1973, my brothers and I were told again that we were going to live with our parents in the United States. My brothers were excited, but I felt sad. I didn't want to go. I didn't want to leave Mama.

Mama was melancholy the day before we left for America. She cried on and off throughout the day. I couldn't understand why Mama was sad. At first, tears lined her cheeks, followed by quiet whimpers and sniffles whenever she looked at me and my brothers. Then, surprisingly, her tears cascaded onto the kitchen floor like Dunn's River Falls into the limpid blue water of the Caribbean Sea.

I ran to her and threw my arms around her waist.

"Mama, don't cry. We'll come back to see you tomorrow," I said, trying to comfort her. My six-year-old self didn't understand that I'd be living two thousand miles away with a sea between us.

"Mama, we're going on that big plane to America."

"I know, baby, it's just that I'm going to miss you so much." That night, I didn't sleep in my regular bed with my aunt. Mama picked me up and laid me in bed with her, Adrian, and Brian. I nestled between Brian and Mama. She hugged the three of us as if she wanted the night to last forever. Then she began to sing:

"My Bonnie lies over the ocean. My Bonnie lies over the sea. My Bonnies lie over the ocean. Will you bring back my Bonnies to me?"

I drifted off to sleep feeling the love that emanated from her voice and her heart. I was in our enchanted world again. I woke up in the middle of the night by Brian's accidental kicks in my lower back as he slept. I pushed his feet towards the wall away from me and heard Mama still singing that Bonnie song.

"Mama, who is Bonnie?" I asked.

"You are. Adrian is, and so is Brian."

"Oh," I replied. I could feel how much she loved us.

That night formed a unique covering of Love on my consciousness that would comfort me when I needed it on my life journey in America. Love was my beginning.

CHAPTER THREE

I Wish I Didn't Live Here

W hen I arrived in the United States to live with my parents, I had my own beautiful room for the first time in my life, which Ms. Brown decorated and filled with lots of toys and clothing. My closet held more dresses than I could wear in a month and shoes with little heels, but very few pants or sneakers. She continued molding me into the daughter she would like.

At first glance, I felt lucky to have gained so much. But that same night, things changed. My parents argued about everything, especially on how to parent us. Besides them arguing, Ms. Brown slapped me in the face numerous times because I kept calling her Fay instead of Mom. I wasn't trying to hurt her nor flout her wishes, but in my six-year-old mind, Mama was my mom, not her. Ms. Brown was my mother but hadn't been my mom since she left me at five and a half months old. Although I was her child, she wasn't ready for a daughter. She wouldn't allow time for us to evolve beyond the compulsory obligations of mother and child to become mom and daughter.

I had moved from my grandparents' dysfunctional home to my parents' dysfunctional home. I went from feeling like the luckiest girl in the world to the saddest within a few hours. My first night was an indication of what my next ten years would be like. My basic living needs would be met, but I had a decade of pain to endure.

One early morning, I was awakened by noises coming from the hallway of our apartment. I got out of bed and peeped out of my bedroom door. Ms. Brown was sorting clothes for laundry day while wiping away tears with the back of her hand. I ran to her and hugged her from behind, trying to comfort her. But she threw my arms from around her waist and shoved me so hard, I almost landed into the wall of the hallway. "Go back to bed," she snapped. I hurried back to my room while trying to regain my balance.

I crawled back into bed and balled up underneath my covers like a turtle retracting into its shell from danger. Ms. Brown's rejection hit me like a ton of bricks, and I wanted to hide from the hurt and shame of it.

I remembered Mama's voice and sang myself back to sleep visualizing myself next to her. "My Bonnie lies over the ocean, my Bonnie lies over the sea…"

Mama was Bonnie now.

At seven years old, my parents gave me the responsibility of looking after Adrian and Brian, who were twenty-one months younger than me. If my brothers did anything wrong, my parents punished or beat me. When Adrian, Brian, and I were young, we had a strict 6 p.m. curfew, and I was responsible for getting us home on time. One day my brothers wouldn't listen to me, and we arrived home late. I tried to explain our tardiness to our father. I told him that Adrian and Brian wouldn't leave with me when I first told them we needed to go home. He said it was my responsibility and I should've made them adhere to the curfew, then he whipped me. I was seven. *How am I supposed to do this?* I thought, confused and afraid to ask.

The next day, the same scenario. To be punctual, I left Adrian and Brian when they wouldn't come with me. My father whipped me again. This time, he told me never to leave them. I didn't know how to win in this situation and many others he held me accountable for.

I continued to be responsible for Adrian and Brian's actions for the next ten years. They were never held accountable for anything, and I was forced to be their caregiver. My father's actions towards me were demeaning and thoughtless. Mostly, he did not acknowledge my presence. He showed favoritism, and I wasn't his favorite. I didn't understand why my father acted this way with me, and Ms. Brown never questioned his methods. My parents were not embodied horizons for me.

I remembered praying with Mama and what she said God could do. All I had to do was ask. So, before falling asleep every night, I prayed to Him. For months, I asked God to send me back to Mama. But nothing happened. I begged and I begged. Nothing happened. I asked Him to show me a sign of his existence. Still, nothing happened. Then one morning I said to God that he was either not real or he lied to Mama about what He can do. I was angry with Him, and told Him that He was not all-powerful and I did not believe in Him. I stopped speaking to God for many years.

I was losing myself. Ms. Brown often steered me away from the things that made me happy. I'd get in trouble if I was reading or romping with Adrian and Brian. She felt I should be doing housework or taking care of my brothers instead. She'd yell, "Go find something around the house to do." I was becoming withdrawn and depressed. Anger was beginning to live within me. I needed a form of relief from the daily pain I was feeling. Since God wasn't helpful, and I'd get in trouble for reading, I started to read underneath my bed with a flashlight when everyone was asleep. There, I could envision my life through stories.

Ms. Brown continued to be unkind and critical of me. She was rarely affectionate and when she was, it was superficially done in the presence of her colleagues and friends. The truth was that

Ms. Brown wasn't a loving, doting mother to me. She doted on her favorite niece and nephew. Her cruelty towards me only increased from my first night in America. She had a negative disposition that sucked the life out of our home. My parents never said they loved me or that they were proud of me. They humiliated, punished, and beat me regularly. Love did not define my life in America and was absent in the middle.

"You freckled face girl," the boys from across the hall yelled at me one day. They and my brothers and I had just stepped off the elevator together to go to our respective apartments.

"Shut up," Brian yelled back.

But the boys continued with the name-calling. After the last warning, a squabble broke out in the hallway between us. The boys' mother heard the commotion and came out of her apartment to break up the fight. She yelled at us and blamed us for what happened.

"You kids are nothing but troublemakers. I'm going to tell your parents," she said, pushing her sons into their apartment.

"We're not troublemakers, and your sons started it," I shouted back.

The lady gave me and my brothers a disgusted look and slammed the door in our faces.

When Ms. Brown got off the elevator that evening, the neighbor heard her walking past her apartment door and confronted her. I heard loud talking in the hall and opened our door to see what was happening. I stood there with my mouth agape as the neighbor spewed lies after lies about the earlier situation with her sons.

My brothers and I tried to interrupt to tell Ms. Brown the truth but she snapped, "Shut up and close the door." When Ms. Brown was done listening to the neighbor, she punished Adrian and Brian by sending them to their rooms until dinner, and then she got the belt and beat me. I was still trying to explain to my mother what really happened, but she wouldn't listen to what I had to say.

Ms. Brown kept asking me, "So, you're telling me that an adult lied on you?"

Every time she asked that question, I would say, "That is not what happened." My voice weakened with each slap of the belt. Ms. Brown would hit me harder each time she asked the question. I eventually stopped trying to defend my brothers and myself. Afterwards, I was told to stay in my room until dinnertime.

I sat at my desk, took my notebook out of my book bag and wrote "ADULTS ARE LIARS," three times across and on every single line. I wrote it until my fingers got tired. When I was done, I laid on my pink carpet and cried some more. I thought about my future children and what I'd do in a scenario like this. Then I got up off the carpet, took out my notebook again, and wrote:

> *I will never listen to adults. I will always listen to my children first because adults are liars. And they are mean. The End.*

I continued to write brief notes about my feelings, home life, and to my future self. I would write, "I'm going to hug my children," "I'll tell them that I love them every day," "I'll tell them that I am proud of them." I would also whisper this same dialogue with my future children to myself when I was alone too. When my parents fought, I would write or say, "I'll never marry a man that speaks to me that way," or "I'll never marry a man that hits me." I did not know this was a form of journaling and of healthy unloading. I was simply trying to release the pain I was feeling. I was hurting so badly and needed the pain to sit on the outside of my body instead of the inside of me. I can't tell you how I knew to do that. I just did it. When I was done expressing, I would throw the notes in the apartment incinerator if my parents weren't home, or I'd hide it in my school bag to throw it in the garbage at school because I'd found out that Ms. Brown searched my room when I wasn't around. I wanted to tell my teachers but was afraid if they confronted Ms. Brown I would be in greater trouble. So, I stayed quiet about my situation.

No one would imagine what was happening at home with me. I was one of the best dressed kids in school. I was flooded with material things and my family had more than most in our Bronx neighborhood. I was living a charmed life. But I was withdrawn and rarely spoke in class for the first couple of years in this country. People chalked it up to me being shy, but I was sad and terrified. Terrified of making a mistake. Terrified of saying the wrong thing. Just terrified.

Ms. Brown's reign of terror reached its peak one Sunday, when I didn't remember to do exactly what she wanted. I was playing with my brothers on the terrace of our apartment when Ms. Brown called me to prep the onions and green bell peppers for the rice and peas she was making for dinner. I hated being called away from having fun to do chores. It seemed like Ms. Brown never wanted me to be happy and simply be. Many times, it felt this was her intention.

An onion, a small green bell pepper, and a knife sat on the wooden cutting board on the counter next to the refrigerator. I began slicing the onions while glancing at my brothers on the terrace who continued on with our version of baseball while awaiting my return. The sun shone brightly through the large window that expanded from the dining room to the living room. We had a panoramic view of the other buildings in the Highbridge area of the Bronx from our sixteenth-floor apartment. I stared out at the grayscale rooftops that stretched for miles of the borough-scape. I released a huge sigh and stopped slicing the onion to take in the beautiful view. Was the horizon trying to get my attention?

Within seconds, my head jerked backwards from a blow to my forehead and the beautiful scenery disappeared as I blinked.

A drop of liquid fell on my eyelashes, then another, then another. I was now seeing the view of the beautiful rooftops as if through red glass.

"I need the onions diced not sliced for the rice and peas," Ms. Brown shouted. I looked down to see that droplets of red colored the vegetables, knife, and cutting board. I dropped the knife and put my hand towards my throbbing forehead. It felt wet. When Ms. Brown saw that I was slicing the onions instead of dicing them, she took the large cook spoon she was stirring the pot on the stove with and hit me so hard in my widow's peak hairline that blood gushed out.

Ms. Brown grabbed a dish towel and placed it on my forehead. Tilting my head back, she quickly ushered me to the bathroom. She opened the medicine chest with one hand and scoured for aid while applying pressure to my forehead with the other. Her hand shook, I think from realizing what she had just done. I didn't cry. I was confused and my head hurt. She dressed my wound and told me to go lie down.

My bedroom was either my refuge or my hell. That day it was my safe haven. It was difficult to comprehend what just happened. I laid on my back and began to shake. Ms. Brown's words reverberated in my head. "I need the onions diced not sliced for the rice and peas." Sometimes, I just didn't understand why.

I was afraid to touch my forehead. I got up slowly and sat on my windowsill, gazing out at a gray sky. It was now drizzling, and without my participation, my brothers had deserted our game. I could hear them bickering in the living room. The world seemed so beautiful. So peaceful. I noticed the different shapes and sizes of the clouds in the distance and wondered what city they were watering. *I wish I didn't live here.* I wanted to live out there, beyond this world, on a cloud even.

I didn't want to think about my forehead, and I was still afraid to touch it. So, I imagined sitting on one of the medium-sized clouds while dangling my feet. I viewed the world from above and it seemed so beautiful. I wanted to sit there forever. Thoughts of

Ms. Brown flooded my head, and I wanted them to go away. *She's not my real mother.* How satisfying that thought felt. *I must be adopted then,* another pleasing thought. More relief. *If she's not my real mother, then I need to find my real mother. I need to find my real family.* Elation replaced my pain. *How exciting,* I thought, and wanted to immediately begin my search. *But how will I do that?*

I came up with a brilliant idea. I pretended I was a superhero with powerful vision. *My superpower will help me find my real family.* I turned my high-beam vision on and scoured the earth searching from my cloud. In a matter of minutes, I found them.

There was a neon sign on their front porch that blinked "Kadian, we miss you." I jumped from my cloud and swooped down using my red cape and landed on their doorstep. I took a deep breath and rang the doorbell. My parents opened the door together and with loving eyes and wide-open smiles said, "Kadian, you found us! We've been looking for you." Then, they hugged me tight and said, "We're so happy you're home. We love you and missed you so much." I stayed with my real family and lived happily ever after and never returned to Mr. and Mrs. Brown. The End.

I'd consume myself in my superhero reverie often to vicariously feel happiness in my childhood. It helped me survive my mother's demands. But it didn't help me contain Charm. She was becoming stronger. She brought forth an angry and resentful person. As these emotions grew within me, I was unaware that they were distancing me from the most important relationship I will ever have—with my soul. The fun and loving parts of me were diminishing as I struggled to maintain the true nature of Kadian and allowed Charm, the angry and aggressive modification, to emerge.

My modification was becoming apparent to others too. When I was ten years old, my parents sent me and my brothers to Jamaica for the entire summer. One afternoon, Mama overheard me say something rude to a neighbor's child and scolded me for it.

Without thinking, I turned away from her, sucked my teeth, and shouted at her, "I don't care."

That was the first time I'd ever spoken to Mama in that manner, and I could feel the wrongness throughout my body almost immediately. I did everything in my power not to cry.

In her stern voice, Mama said, "Charm, come to me." But I wouldn't. I just turned in her direction with my face down.

"Come to me, I said," demanded Mama again.

I was too ashamed to move. I just stood there and kept my face down. I'd never been disobedient or disrespectful to her before.

"Who are you?" she asked sternly.

I am Charm, I said in my mind but not out loud. I didn't remember Kadian.

"Who are you?" Mama repeated her question to me. Once again, I didn't answer. I stood there with my head down and shrugged my shoulders. A tower of shame filled my body.

"You must remember who you are Charm. You are not like everyone else."

Standing there with my head down, I asked, "Can I go now?"

I could feel her stare of disappointment like when I lit the room on fire, but I didn't dare look up. I felt too ashamed. When she did not respond to my question after a few seconds, I walked away. I sat on the steps on the side of the house and bawled my eyes out. I had hurt Mama and felt deeply sorry. I don't know why I didn't apologize to her because I really wanted to.

Mama died a year after that incident. It was in January 1979, and I was eleven years old. Her death devastated me and my brothers. When my parents broke the news to us, we fell to the floor in my brothers' room and wept while holding each other. It was the worst news of our lives. When I first arrived in this country, I slept in my brothers' room for about a year even though I had my own room. We were not used to being apart, so the first few nights my parents would find me there in the morning. They gave up trying to get me to sleep in my own room and allowed me to sleep in my brothers' room in one of the twin beds, with Adrian and Brian in the other. As soon as my father turned the lights out, Adrian and Brian would get in the bed with me and the three of us slept holding each other. Sometimes, it seemed like we were triplets.

The night my parents told us Mama died, I got out of my bed and went to Adrian and Brian's room to sleep. We put the beds together and the three of us slept holding each other. When my father opened my brothers' room door in the morning, I heard him say, "Fay, here she is. Come look." He wanted my mother to see the three of us slumbering in bed together. My parents were told that Mama's last words were, "Charm, Adrian, and Brian" and then she left this planet.

We flew to Jamaica for the funeral. One afternoon following Mama's funeral, a squabble occurred between my brothers, two cousins, and myself. One of my cousins said to Ms. Brown that I started it. It was untrue. I told Ms. Brown the truth. "I didn't start it, she did."

I could tell that Ms. Brown knew I was telling the truth, but she wanted to humiliate me. She retrieved one of my father's belts from the bedroom and struck me. I felt a sharp pain across my neck. Ms. Brown continued to beat me in front of my brothers, cousins, aunts, uncles, uncles' girlfriends, and friends over something I did not do. It was the most humiliating day of my life. When Ms. Brown was done, she sent me to bed, and I cried myself to sleep.

I woke up crying. I had welts all over my arms, legs, back, and neck. I looked in the bathroom mirror and felt so ashamed. Beaten for something I did not do and shamed in front of everyone, I went back in the bedroom and continued crying. One of my uncles' girlfriends entered the room when she heard me whimpering and said, "Someone eventually told the truth and said it was not you," and then added, "Charm, sometimes we get in trouble for other people's wrongs. That's just life." But I didn't just get in trouble for someone else's wrong. Ms. Brown decided to take her niece's words over her own daughter's even though she knew I was telling the truth. Ms. Brown had a choice, and she never chooses me.

This beating incident in Jamaica would cement a wall between Ms. Brown and me, separating us. It would block whatever love, trust, and forgiveness might try to seep through, leading to more dysfunction for years to come.

When I sat up in the bed, I couldn't hold onto who I was at the core anymore. I could feel the shutting down of that gleeful little girl who loved to romp and enjoy life. She wanted what any child would want from their parents: love and attention. She simply wanted to please them and make them proud, but she slowly withered away. That was Kadian, the authentic me and the connector to my soul.

When the anger inside me exploded, a new and unidentifiable modified version of me emerged. Charm had fully manifested due to Ms. Brown's unkind words and actions, and, without Mama's help to keep me aligned at my core, my modification completed itself. Charm was more than her family's moniker—she would become their creation.

The first night in the United States created a path that I would walk for many years. A path that mimicked parts of my parents' lives and the many patterns and beliefs I would take on. Instead of gaining a happy new life, a journey of losses ensued. I lost authentic happiness. I lost Kadian. I lost connection with my soul. When I landed in the United States, I no longer had any embodied horizons to continue watering the seeds planted within me of who I really was. Gradually, my true nature became hidden from me and caged, leaving only a fraction of my true essence. The key to finding my wholeness again was trapped in the depths of my being, in a place where no human had gone nor could go. What could save me now?

I was now Charm. Even though I could periodically feel the two contrasting aspects of myself, Charm was mostly in control. It remained that way for over thirty years until I embarked on a relentless pursuit of authentic happiness, hoping to find my true self again. It was not an easy quest, but rediscovering and reclaiming myself was worth every step I took, every path I ventured on, every person I encountered, and every experience I had. It has all taught me about the magnitude of my strength and the measure of my courage. I saw my persistence and resilience within that refused to settle for a life designed for me by others. I was determined to live the life my soul carved out for me before I jumped into my mother's womb.

CHAPTER FOUR

Get Out!

I can only imagine waking up one morning at five-and-a-half months old without the comfort of my mother's breast, the loss of her voice, the disappearance of her scent. I'm certain my modifications began here. My parents' absence in my early life carved out a lifelong disconnection between me and Ms. Brown and left me with a relationship that never developed with my father. I have almost no memory of him before the age of seven.

As a child, I wasn't in control of my life. There was nothing I could do about my situation, and it was difficult to stop the changes I felt happening within. I tried to remember who I was, like Mama told me to, but containing Charm was impossible in my current environment. My parents' home mimicked the violent home in Jamaica. How many of us are born to parents who are walking embodiments of the person their family created?

Growing up, everything was decided for me. I had no input nor was ever asked my opinion about my own life. I was raised in the era of "children are seen and not heard," and my family adhered to that and made it a belief system. That was how it was in my culture—total parental control and dominance.

Over the years, my parents' marriage deteriorated. So did my relationship with them. When I was seventeen, my parents, twin brothers, one of my half-sisters, my half-brother, and I went to Jamaica on vacation. Two of my two half-sisters still lived there.

The trip excited me at first, but that changed shortly after we arrived. My parents fought more than usual, and every day a different family drama materialized. The idea of a fun-filled vacation disappeared quickly. I was under constant surveillance by my father, given that I was an adolescent and male interactions were forbidden. This led to more restrictions than usual for me. My parents, Adrian, Brian, and I returned home while my half-brother and half-sister remained. I was happy to leave, but not my twin brothers, who'd had a ball given all the freedom granted to them.

When the five of us stepped off the Air Jamaica plane and ended our summer vacation of 1984, we didn't know this would be a turning point for all of us.

At first, it was a relief to be home. I would be entering my senior year of high school the following week and I felt kind of excited about that. Ms. Brown took me shopping for school supplies and new clothes as she did every year. When we returned around 9:30 p.m., my father was sitting in the living room fuming because I had left the house without his permission, even though I'd gone with my mother. He shouted, "I don't care who you left the house with. Get out of my house!"

His reaction shocked and confused me. It was nonsensical. The ferocity of his tone made it seem like I had done something reprehensible. But when it came to me, nothing made sense with my father. I wasn't going to argue or beg to stay. As a matter of fact, I felt relieved.

An argument ensued between my parents. I can scarcely recall Ms. Brown ever defending me. I sat in my room and listened to them argue for a while. When my father realized I hadn't left, he entered my room, went into my closet, and began throwing my clothes on the floor. "Get out!" he shouted again, with a look of disdain. He then flounced back to the living room and resumed arguing with Ms. Brown. Ms. Brown insisted that I stay, and my father demanded that I leave. Ms. Brown did not know that I had already sided with my father. I had had enough.

I grabbed a small bag from my closet and packed it with only necessities while trying to figure out where I would go. After the small bag was full, I put it on the floor next to my bedroom door and grabbed my new school bag. I filled it with the school supplies Ms. Brown bought me when we went shopping and whatever clothing I could fit.

I sat on my bed and listened to my parents in this heated argument, wondering who was going to win. But it didn't matter because my mind was already made up. I wasn't staying.

My father entered my room again to see if I was done packing. "Why are you still here?" he asked angrily.

"I'm packing my stuff," I replied with equal anger. He glanced at the bags by my door, sighed, and stomped towards the living room to continue the unabated argument with his wife. I picked the largest purse I had in my closet and began filling it with items I might need. I grabbed my toothbrush from the bathroom and an extra toothpaste from the cabinet. Then I checked my wallet. I only had a couple of bucks. It wasn't enough to get me by taxi to any of the destinations that I had in mind. It was now almost midnight. I was afraid to take public transportation, but I didn't have a choice.

I decided to go to my half-brother's apartment in Mount Vernon, New York. He lived with his girlfriend and my half-sister. I felt afraid because it was over an hour's bus ride from where I lived in the Bronx. I had enough money to get there by the city's public transportation, which operated on a 24-hour schedule, but not enough for a taxi to my brother's place when I arrived in Mount Vernon. Public transportation ceases in Mount Vernon around 8 p.m. Also, my half-brother and half-sister were still in Jamaica, and I was unsure if his girlfriend was home. They did not have a working phone so I couldn't call to confirm. "I'll just have to walk very fast," I thought to myself. If she wasn't home, I would go to my uncle's apartment, which was about three miles from my brother's apartment. He, too, did not have a working phone. I sat on my bed, ironing out my plan in my head while listening to my parents' marathon argument. It was getting late so I threw my purse over my right shoulder, my school bag over my left shoulder, and with the small bag in my right hand, I went towards the front door. While waiting for the elevator, I heard the door to our apartment open. Ms. Brown hurried towards me and handed me twenty dollars. She said to be careful and dashed back to the apartment.

The elevator arrived. I got in and pressed L for lobby. I looked at the twenty-dollar bill in my hand with a sigh of relief. I could take a taxi to my brother's apartment, and if no one was home, I could ask the taxi driver to take me to my uncle's place. The elevator reached the lobby and opened its doors to a new path, riddled with many unknowns and uncertainties. I walked out of the building where I had lived for almost eleven years with a smile on my face. I was free.

I crossed the street to wait for the BX37 bus. It was now after midnight. All businesses in the neighborhood were closed; no one was around. I stood at the bus stop and listened to the deafening silence of that hour. Silence's ominous presence crept from my feet, shot through my legs, and settled in my gut. The fast rhythm of my heartbeat disturbed the silence, informing me of how afraid I was. My eyes welled up with tears as the seriousness of my situation became real for me. Looking up at the building towards the sixteenth floor, I saw Ms. Brown standing on the terrace of the apartment, waiting for me to get on the bus.

I didn't have to wait long for the bus to arrive. *Good timing*, I thought. I wiped my tears, waved goodbye to Ms. Brown, and waited for the bus to stop in front of me. But I hesitated when the door slid open. There were no passengers on the bus, and I remembered the girl in my junior high school who was fondled by a bus driver when she was alone with him. My heart was now pounding. I held my breath, held back the tears, and walked onto the bus. I set my bags down and dug in my purse for the seventy-five cents fare I knew I didn't have. I only had the twenty-dollar bill Ms. Brown gave me and the couple of dollars I found in my purse earlier but no change. I had forgotten that I would need change for the bus. I shook my purse in hopes of hearing some magical coins jiggle about, but no such miracle occurred. Panic overtook me, and the tears that I was holding back shattered my composure as I looked towards the open door. I reached for my bags to exit the bus when the front door slid close. "Have a seat and don't worry about the fare," said the bus driver.

Feeling grateful for my miracle, I thanked him, picked up my bags, and sat a few rows behind him. I began devising a protective plan in my head. I placed my small handbag on the floor and put my school bag on top of it. I positioned them where the bus driver would have to step over them to get to me. I sat two seats away from my bags which gave me ample time to run to the middle exit door to depart the bus if necessary. But I didn't have to execute my escape plan. The bus driver sensed my fear and tried to dispel it by first telling me his name was Bernard. He asked me a few questions, and a conversation transpired. Bernard was shocked to see me by myself at that hour. He expressed sympathy towards my situation and his disgust with my father. I felt safe with him but still sat on the side of caution.

This bus ride lasted about fifteen minutes. I had to transfer to the BX11 bus that would take me to the border of the Bronx and Mount Vernon. When we arrived at the transfer stop, Bernard told me to stay on the bus and he'd wait for the BX11 to arrive. He didn't want me waiting by myself at that hour of the morning. We waited and continued with our conversation. When the BX11 arrived, he knew the bus driver. Bernard explained what happened to me and told him to make sure I got to my destination safely. The other bus driver said, "Certainly."

I thanked Bernard for being so kind, and he handed me a bus transfer with a slight nod. I smiled. We exchanged no more words. His duty was over. Bernard had taken hold of my destiny when he closed the door to his bus and told me to have a seat. I believe he understood what it meant to be a momentary fate-keeper. He held my path close to his heart with care and honor. He made decisions in our brief encounter to ensure my safety. If only my father had honored my destiny with the same level of care as this stranger.

I boarded the BX11 bus, handed the driver my bus transfer, and put in place my original plan to be safe, just in case. I positioned my bags on the floor and sat a couple of seats away. We were alone for about fifteen minutes before another passenger came on. People were getting on and off the bus until about the last twenty minutes of the ride. Then we were alone again. He asked me how I was going to get to my destination, given public transportation in Mount Vernon was out of service for a few hours and the taxi stands were closed. I'd known that bus service wasn't available, but I hadn't known that the taxi stands were closed. When he saw my concerned look, he asked if someone was meeting me. I said, "No. I'll walk."

We arrived at the last stop around 1:30 a.m. The bus driver wished me well and told me to be safe. I got off the bus and looked around 241st. It was dark and deserted, with a resounding silence that overwhelmed me again. I secured my bags around my neck, shoulder, and in my hand, and took off at full pelt towards my half-brother's house. I ran and prayed. I prayed for stamina. I prayed that someone would be at my brother's place. I asked Mama to keep me safe. I didn't stop running until I got to my destination.

I rang the doorbell and waited. No one answered. Being almost out of breath, I dropped my bags and banged on the door in desperation from the burden of the last few hours of my life, which weighed heavily on my shoulders now. I was about to bawl my eyes out when a light came on. I sighed in relief. A cousin opened the door and looked at me, bewildered. She tried to look behind me before asking me how I got there. I summarized what happened and how I ran all the way from 241st. She helped me with my bags as she expressed her displeasure with my father's (her uncle's) actions. My cousin and I talked briefly. Afterwards, I went to my half-sister's room and prepared for bed. I was exhausted but grateful to have arrived safely. I whispered, "Thank you," and fell asleep.

I called Ms. Brown every day for about a week, but my father hung up whenever he heard my voice. After another week of wearing the same clothing over and over, I decided to go to the apartment for more of my things, but my father wouldn't give them to me and slammed the door in my face. Feeling defeated and sad, I started walking towards the train station to return to Mount Vernon when an anger rose up in me. I immediately turned in the opposite direction and sprinted to the police station to tell them my dilemma.

A police officer drove me back to the apartment to speak with my father. On the way there, the officer listened to my story in detail from where I sat in the back seat of the patrol car. He tried to convince me to go back home, feeling I was too young to be on my own. He said he thought that if there was a chance to patch things up with my father, I should do so.

When we arrived at the apartment, my father told the police officer loads of untruths, saying I could come back if I wished because he wanted me back. He was trying to convince the officer he was a good father and everything was a misunderstanding. He was putting on such a show. But I wasn't convinced. I said no to the officer, took my clothes, and left. I'd had enough of my father's mental and verbal abuse. Freedom was the gift Life had granted me and I was grateful.

Oftentimes a gift doesn't come wrapped with a bow but is a beautiful beginning cloaked in a tragic encounter. I had to look past this tragedy and connect to my true feelings about the situation to see the beautiful present. This gift felt good, deep down in my being, even though I had no money, job, guidance, or home.

At least I was free of my father. I was finally able to breathe after ten years of living in a dysfunctional, abusive, and chaotic home. This decision changed the course of my life. Even though I didn't have a clue as to where my life was coursing, I consciously chose myself, and I am so glad I did.

I never lived with my father ever again. It would take years to want a relationship with him and decades to consider forgiving him. I was free of my father's cruel intentions towards me and the many years of feeling powerless and in pain. I was homeless, but I could live my own life and make my own decisions. I was physically free, but parts of my soul still remained encased by the damage from my childhood.

One thing I knew for certain, I was never going to give him control of me again. I would learn how to weave in and out of his world and maintain who I was becoming. After that night and over the years, I learned a new empowered way to relate to my father, but removing myself from my mother's reality took longer. There were greater lessons to be learned and a higher calling to be heard while I continued to rendezvous in Ms. Brown's world.

About three months later, my father walked away from his marriage and went to Jamaica to live with the woman he was having an affair with. My father's sudden absence was shocking, and difficult for Adrian and Brian because they were the apples of his eye. They turned to drugs to soothe themselves and eventually dropped out of high school.

For almost a year, I bounced from place to place, trying not to be a burden to people. I stayed at my half-brother's apartment, then when things got uncomfortable, I'd go to my uncle's place. When things got weird there, I stayed with friends or my boyfriend. I went to school every day. School was an escape from my personal troubles. But it was getting difficult to attend because I couldn't afford the train rides. I stayed in Mount Vernon, but my school was located by the Brooklyn Bridge in Manhattan. I had to take the Metro-North Commuter Railroad to New York City and transfer to the New York city subway trains, a costly hour-long commute. I began stowing away on the Metro-North train line and found myself jumping the turnstile in New York City to get to school. But I was becoming afraid of getting caught. And, with my father gone, Ms. Brown called me at school often because Adrian and Brian were misbehaving. I was mentally and physically drained. I was broke and alone. I was not myself.

I was at the end of my rope and about to drop out of high school when I confided in two of my teachers about my situation. My English teacher, Ms. Hazzard, offered to give me a ride to school in the mornings. She lived in Yonkers, the town over from Mount Vernon. I rode with Ms. Hazzard to school for the remainder of the school year. Maria, my computer-lab teacher, gave me a job at the high school in the evenings as her assistant teacher so I could take care of myself financially. I taught word processing for the adult education school alongside Maria, Mondays through Thursdays from 5 to 9 p.m. These few air pockets saved my life while I was drowning because of two embodied horizons who surprisingly sprang into action to help me.

A couple of months later, a cousin informed me her employer, RGIS, was hiring for the Christmas holiday, so I applied. RGIS hired me as an inventory specialist on the weekends. After the holidays, I was hired as a temp. I worked alternating Friday evenings and every weekend. I stayed mostly in Mount Vernon, attended Murry Bergtraum High School in Manhattan, and held down two jobs. Thanks to two caring human beings, Ms. Hazzard and Maria, I received my high school diploma.

About six weeks after graduating, I moved in with Ms. Brown when she bought her first home. I was finally feeling safe and enjoying my own room again. I worked and took care of myself. But that was short-lived. About four weeks later, Ms. Brown gave me an ultimatum. I had to either go to college or leave her house.

I didn't understand how the idea of college came about, given no prior discussion on the subject. Later on, I found out that my cousin was starting at Cheyney University in Pennsylvania, and Ms. Brown wanted me to enroll there.

Feeling afraid of being homeless again, I packed my things, brought my high school transcript and other personal information, and plopped down next to my cousin in her father's car while Ms. Brown sat in the front seat. On the way there, I had mixed feelings. My high school counselor had thought I could get into a decent college with my grades, but after my father threw me out, I could only focus on my survival and my grades slipped. I had thought that college wouldn't be an option for me anymore, but that day I enrolled at Cheyney, and my cousin and I became dorm mates. I didn't know what to major in. Not knowing what I wanted to do with the rest of my life added to my dilemma. Since computer science was my core concentration in high school and given the direction the world seemed to be headed, I picked computer science for my major, but without enthusiasm.

Watching Ms. Brown and my uncle drive away when they left me at college, I felt a sudden awareness that happiness wasn't what I thought it was. I had never wondered about happiness because my parents had taught me that material things were happiness. My programmed perceptions began very early on—I had a lot of material things growing up. Alone in the dorm room, I showered and laid on my bed, closed my eyes, and cried.

An immense anger erupted inside because being at college was not my choice. I had other plans for my life. I wanted to continue working, to save more money to travel. I wanted to help the less fortunate. I wanted to explore this planet. I wanted experiences that my upbringing hadn't afforded me. I did not want to be stuck on a campus focusing on a degree I was not excited about.

Those feelings were a glimmer of Kadian forcing her way through my anger to remind me of who I really was at the core of my being. She wasn't completely gone. But I was facing a familiar actuality once again, and all the fears that came with it. If I left school, I would be homeless again. So, I stayed.

I met my future husband, Marlon, the night after my family left me at college. I was eighteen and he was twenty. Marlon had arrived in America from Jamaica on a student visa with a scholarship to play soccer at Cheyney University. I met him at an off-campus party my cousin and I attended. It turned out we had a class together that first semester. We saw each other a lot around campus and had a liking for each other, but once again I could only focus on my survival, which left almost no room for a potentially serious relationship. That's because nothing had really changed in my personal life when I was at college. I had to figure my own way through things, and Ms. Brown continued calling me about Adrian and Brian and their issues. Marlon and I started dating our second year of college in 1986.

During my college years, Adrian and Brian were the beneficiaries of my parents' attention, time, and money. My parents' finances were spent on lawyers for their many offenses. I received no financial help from my father and very little from Ms. Brown. Even with grants and loans, I still had a tuition balance every year.

Two more surprising embodied horizons saved me from drowning. I was granted work study with Coach Hinson, the athletic director and Mrs. Miller, his secretary, for financial assistance. Coach Hinson awarded me with scholarships on a few occasions to subsidize my tuition. He and Mrs. Miller fed me and provided for me when I had no funds to support myself. Working with them yielded opportunities that resulted in multiple streams of income to further pay for tuition and books, and to take care of myself during my years at Cheyney University. I am a college graduate because of them. During my college years, my presence at home became sparse. I stayed on campus, did internships, and visited with friends.

One day towards the end of my third year of college, I was in

Marlon's dorm room feeling irritated by his presence and insti-
gated a fight with him. I slammed his room door and stormed
down the stairs. Suddenly, I became dizzy and fainted. One of
Marlon's teammates happened to be coming up the stairs and
caught me. When I woke up, I was laying on Marlon's bed. Marlon
thought lack of eating had caused my spell so he left to get me
food.

I fell asleep while he was gone and dreamt that I was sitting on
my family's verandah in Jamaica when Mama appeared. We were
so happy to see each other. She hugged me then took my face in
her hands and said, "Everything is going to be all right. You don't
have to worry." Then she kissed me on the forehead and walked
away. I opened my eyes to see Marlon unpacking what he'd bought
for me.

Two weeks after arriving home at the end of the semester, my
aunt noticed that my breasts had grown and said I should take a
pregnancy test. I didn't think one was necessary because I was on
birth control pills, still having my menstrual cycle, and had no
symptoms. I couldn't see how pregnancy was possible, but I took
the test anyway. It was positive.

At the end of June, I went to the clinic just to be sure because I
was preparing to go away to my internship at AT&T. They
confirmed I was indeed with child. After explaining I was on birth
control, they asked if I'd taken any other medication. I remembered I was prescribed antibiotics a few months earlier for a
terrible flu. They said it was possible that the antibiotics interfered
with the birth control pills. My first child, Kamilah, saw an opportunity to jump into my birth canal and conceal herself, like I did in
Ms. Brown's womb.

Marlon told Ms. Brown, and she said I should have an abortion
so I could finish school. Marlon vehemently said no, that he would
stay home with the baby and allow me to graduate if it came to
that. The clinic called a week or so later, wanting me to come in to
take a blood test because the doctor noticed when he did a pelvic
exam that my uterus hadn't grown and a due date could not be

determined since I was still on my menstrual cycle. The blood test showed I was much further along than they thought—possibly four to four-and-a-half months. They decided to retest me in case something happened with the first test. I went back to the clinic in early July. Being so far along perplexed the doctor. When he checked the heartbeat, it was loud and very fast. He told me I was going to have a girl, for in his thirty years of experience, girls' heartbeats are fast. I don't think he meant to blurt that out.

They settled on me being about three-and-a-half months pregnant and predicted my due date as the first week in January 1989. This was perfect because I would be home for winter break and could finish my last semester.

For the rest of the summer, I went to my intern program in New Jersey. I decided not to let the coordinators know I was pregnant for fear of losing the internship. I stayed on the Rutgers University campus for the entire program, did not have any symptoms, and was able to keep my pregnancy hidden because my belly still wasn't growing.

I went back to Cheyney University to begin my senior year since I wasn't due until January. Marlon and I decided that I would stay home with our baby for the spring semester, so Marlon could finish. When he graduated, I would finish my last semester. But Kamilah decided otherwise.

Family patterns show up in the strangest of places and in the oddest ways. I wouldn't know until I was writing this memoir that Ms. Brown's surprise discovery of being pregnant with me was so eerily similar to my own. Besides the absence of pregnancy symptoms between us, becoming a mother was not the vision for our lives. Ms. Brown wanted to continue on with her education, and I also had other desires. I wonder why Kamilah and I both decided to interfere with our mothers' trajectory. Did we want to help break generational patterns? Did we want to help our mothers choose their souls? Some might say there is karma to resolve.

My mother wanted to keep her pregnancy. To be honest, I'm not sure I would have kept my baby if I had been more in tune with who I really was at the core. Maybe I would've had the courage to follow through with my true desires instead of beginning a family. But just like I didn't give Ms. Brown a choice, Kamilah didn't give me one either. We left school at the end of the semester on December 16, 1988. Kamilah arrived two days later.

Because Kamilah arrived early, Marlon and I could both graduate, which we did together in May 1989 with Kamilah in attendance. My family insisted we get married. "It's the right thing to do. He's such a nice guy." Deep down, I didn't want to be married. I wanted to be with someone I was in love with. Even though I loved Marlon, I was not in love. I never dreamt about walking down the aisle wearing a white gown. Growing up, I didn't dream about having children. Except for writing notes to my future children when I was angry about my own mother, I didn't spend my days dreaming about having kids. That was the reverie of most of the women in my family. Unfortunately, this fairy tale is sold as happiness to a lot of women in this world. It always felt shallow to me. I still remember playing Barbies with a childhood friend. We would take turns creating a story about our future lives. Her story included getting married, having children, and being in a nice house. Barbie and Ken routinely sat in the house watching television or laying in the bedroom. Her fantasy was so boring to me. When it was my turn to create my story, I put Barbie in the driver's seat of her car and filled the car with my other girl Barbie dolls. I'd tell stories of exploring the world together. Ken was never in the car. When I looked over at my friend, she seemed uninterested and bored.

After graduation, Marlon and I moved our family in with Ms. Brown and my twin brothers. Ms. Brown's house was an open invitation for her family members to come and live and do as they please. Her brothers, sister, nieces, and their significant others lived there on and off and for months at a time. This went on for many years.

A month later, Marlon and I were married with only my mother, grandmother, my best friend, and Marlon's brother and sister-in-law present. I was not interested in a traditional wedding at all. I didn't realize how long "til death do us part" was because I was way too young, and so was he.

While living in Ms. Brown's home, I was the only one who contributed to her household financially. I paid the electricity and phone bill. I bought groceries weekly for everyone. I also had my own personal bills to take care of such as my school loan and taking care of our daughter. That was not enough for Ms. Brown, and she often pressured me to contribute more while everyone else did whatever they wanted with their money. While Marlon applied for permanent residency, he stayed home with Kamilah until he was granted permission to work. I was seldom happy in Ms. Brown's home due to Adrian and Brian's lifestyle and other family members living there. I decided we needed to move out.

In 1990, I began taking a hard look at my life. I wasn't able to save much money. My family's drama interfered with our marriage also. I felt drained mentally. I often felt unhappy. In September 1991, as unhappiness continued to plague me, I left Ms. Brown's home with Marlon and Kamilah, this time of my own volition. I left feeling the way I have always felt about Ms. Brown and our relationship—insignificant compared to my twin brothers and the rest of her family, whom she often put before me. I left feeling like an outsider and a stranger to my own biological mother.

Marlon and I moved into our own apartment in New Jersey. I was now within close proximity of my job, which saved significantly on gas and tolls, among the other things I took care of in Ms. Brown's house. Also, Kamilah would be going to school soon, and I wanted her to be in a better educational system than what I grew up with in the Bronx. At first, I thought moving away from my family would fix my unhappiness, but it did not.

I had a different vision for my life. So did Marlon. He wanted to be a professional soccer player in Europe. Ms. Brown, too, had had a different vision for her life when she was seventeen. We all got thrown off our trajectories. Some people willfully adjust to their new pathway and ignore the calling of the horizon. But it would prove difficult for me to ignore the horizon and the beckoning of my soul.

CHAPTER FIVE

Landing in Depression's Cold, Dark Room

Our move provided a necessary relief from the chaotic milieu of Ms. Brown's house. Marlon and I were jubilant, but Kamilah struggled with being apart from her grandmother. There were no longer daily hugs and kisses or a staircase to slide down on her belly to greet her at the door. Kamilah assigned herself as the phone monitor and ran to pick it up before the first ring ended. "Jandma!" Kamilah always answered with a broad smile, then quickly frowned if a different voice replied. She and Ms. Brown adored each other. It was difficult to watch Kamilah struggle without daily physical access to her grandma, but she soon adjusted to her new life with friends and thrived in school.

I loved our new environment—a quiet suburb in central New Jersey garlanded with greenery. Far contrast from the high-rise buildings where I had lived for almost eleven years; the busy, noisy streets of the Bronx that never slept. Marlon and I both worked for Fortune 500 companies and began acquiring lots of material goods. We filled our two-bedroom apartment with beautiful furniture, and I bought my dream car, a gold Acura Legend coupe.

Working five minutes away from our new apartment gave me the chance to explore our surroundings during my lunch hour.

Periodically, I'd drop by farms and visit with the horses and other farm animals. I admired the gaggle of geese with their goslings strutting in the neighborhood, their pride on display. I loved looking at the deer laying on the lawns as if they too were on a lunch break. I drove into the hills of the town to admire the homes and look down at the townscape. I imagined how beautiful it must be after a snowfall or during the holidays. I'd stare into the horizon, remembering the beach breeze, and fall prey to its bigness and the possibilities it represented.

On occasion, I took Kamilah into the hills to enjoy the view. She'd run around the picnic table with me in pursuit. Then she would sit with me and become preoccupied with her dangling feet. I wondered what her two-year-old mind thought about whenever she looked towards the horizon. Did she sense a greater sense of herself as I did at the beach? The lure of its possibilities brought me there, time and time again.

Marlon and I were excited by the news of our second pregnancy in early 1992. A new life, a toddler, and work occupied most of my attention. I stopped visiting with the horizon and began planning for our future arrival. But, four weeks into my pregnancy, I suffered a miscarriage. It never crossed my mind that miscarriage could happen to me. A profound sadness enshrouded my world that seemed unrelated to my disappointment, though I couldn't name it at the time. For a while, it wouldn't go away. Marlon and I decided to try to have another baby. We received the good news in April 1993, and a month later, we bought our own home.

We were walking billboards advertising the American dream. It was as if our lives were displayed in a panoramic view at Times Square for onlookers to see the duplicitous dream of happiness. On one billboard we promoted our good-paying corporate jobs, dressed in business attire holding attaché cases. Another billboard, adorned with running red, white, and blue lights, would feature us having dinner in our beautifully furnished home. Passersby envied our vacation photos rotating in a slide show. Life seemed picture perfect at twenty-six years old.

Marlon and I continued setting goals and exceeding each one. He loved our manifested world and bought into it wholeheartedly. However, on my drive to work most mornings, I did not feel happy. I only felt successful. Our lives were a clone of our surroundings, everyone creating similar realities and appearances of happiness. Deep down, I felt it should be a unique experience. To me, happiness is the purple house in a community of beige houses. I lived in a beige house, wanting it to be purple. The American dream felt questionable, and I remained noncommittal.

When I wasn't looking toward the horizon, my life seemed small and confined. I had reached a level of success in my life, and gaining more possessions did not appeal to me like the lure of the horizon. I crossed paths with that six-year-old immigrant again who had gained so much, but in truth had lost something more valuable.

The old adage "Money can't buy happiness" traveled through time on a doormat and landed at my front door, reminding me that possessions weren't fulfilling my daily going outs and coming ins. Not quite understanding what was happening to me in my young adulthood, I tried to cure my emptiness by replacing it with more shopping. Shopping helped me to cope briefly, but then it became an addiction.

Shortly after moving into our new home, I suffered my second miscarriage. I was devastated. I was taking the essential steps to bring my storybook's vision of happiness to fruition, but now it seemed incomplete. I soon realized that I was the protagonist *and* the antagonist in my own storybook of happiness. Charm, my inner protagonist, was creating a storyline based on what she and society perceived happiness to be, while Kadian, my inner antagonist, yearned for something more. I would feel Kadian's nudges and turn away from them. Kadian remembered the horizon and called for Charm's attention.

As the protagonist, Charm made promises with Marlon to grow

old together. *We'll buy an RV and drive around the country when we retire.* She liked that dream and wanted to continue striving for it with him, but Kadian, the antagonist, despised it. She had questions. *Is that what you want? Do you want to grow old with Marlon? What would your conversations be like?* In David Whyte's poem "Sometimes," he conveys that we will arrive at a place in our lives that provokes us with profound questions to challenge our current path. He says these are "questions that have no right to go away."

I was at that place, questioning my life trajectory, part of me lying to Marlon and to myself. There were days I could not envision the dream of growing old together. It was slowly vanishing into the vastness. But Charm was still in control and determined to complete her picture of happiness. So, Marlon and I decided to try a third time for another baby.

Our son, Khaleel, was born in November 1994. I was grateful for a healthy baby, and Marlon was overjoyed by having his son. My storybook was completing itself, but I struggled to see a happy ending. I couldn't shrug off the sadness that sat by my bedside after giving birth. The truth was I really didn't want the life I was creating. I wanted to stop creating it and stop who I was becoming. I didn't know how to do so without hurting the people I loved. I was living a charmed life, but whose charmed life?

I decided to take tiny steps towards change. First, I said no more often when my co-workers ask me to out to lunch. Instead, I sat at my desk and ate lunch while I journaled or walked, or moved my car to the far end of Lucent Technologies' parking lot, rolled the windows down, and ate my lunch alone. Then, I'd recline my seat and gaze into the sky.

One lunch hour sitting in my car, I closed my eyes to try envisioning a different life. A few minutes into my fantasy, I heard a strange tone. It sounded like a television that had lost its signal. It didn't sound like anything in nature that I knew of, and I thought I was imagining it. But it didn't cease. I sat with it for a minute then powered up my car window to hear it better. Just then it disappeared. That evening I asked Marlon if he had ever had this experience. He said no. I tried to reproduce the sound by sitting in silence and closing my eyes, but I couldn't. I didn't know how to summon it.

My time alone incited paying close attention to my co-workers, friends, and family members in this middle-class dome we were all sheltered under. They too seemed unhappy despite their achievements. Our complaints, questions, and regrets floated upward and graffitied the shield of our dome, keeping our makeshift snow globe free of outside influences from the horizon. Most people did not look up, afraid of acknowledging their thoughts. But my inner antagonist often interrupted my story with questions to give me pause, forcing my eyeballs upward seeking my horizon. *Why aren't people happy? Why can't I find my life purpose and feel passionate about anything? Why can't I get up every day smiling? What does intimacy feel like and why don't I have it in my marriage?* The antagonist of our story will trigger our own provocative questions, compelling us to bend our own necks back in search of what's beckoning us.

I awoke one morning in 1995 with my seven-hundred-dollar designer handbag staring me in the face. I was repulsed by its presence. I gaped at my bedroom and its expensive furniture with repugnance. I wandered around my home, looked out at my yard, and loathed everything I had. The things in my life were pathetic replicas of happiness. And my unhappiness unmasked their true representation. No magic existed anywhere in my home because I lived in a beige house. Happiness can't be inauthentic.

I made myself a cup of tea and sat in my living room to let the awareness soak in. What I desired was deeper and beyond my scope of understanding. Right then, I made a commitment to investigate this new perspective.

I wanted to explore the questions posed by my inner antagonist about my unpassionate life. In order to do that, I had to leave our snow globe somehow. I decided I'd go to a hotel for the weekend. That didn't go over well with Marlon, who took it personally and as a sign I didn't want to be with him. He didn't understand that I suffered in the space between my modified self and my soul. This affliction wasn't easy to explain to anyone in my life then. They wouldn't understand that a version of me called from the horizon frequently, arousing my curiosity, and when I turned from it, it pained me. Even though the questions of my inner antagonist scared me, I had to satisfy my own curiosity, even if it meant that Marlon would be furious. So, on that Friday after work, I went to the hotel closest to home.

At the hotel, I took a deep breath and closed my eyes. After a few more breaths, my excitement about being away from my busy life began slipping away. The quietness revealed a sadness that had been forming since I landed in this country and had worsened over time. I wanted to cry. I couldn't see this sadness in my busyness, but taking a break from my storybook life revealed what was truly lying beneath its surface. I sat with my feelings but couldn't handle that amount of despair all at once, so I decided to journal like I did as a child to find relief.

After journaling, I found myself imagining what life would be like if I wasn't married. Where I would go. What I'd be doing. My imagination made me feel alive again. And when I was done imagining, I was sad again. The life I was living had taken parts of my soul captive and tethered them to this reality. *How do I set my soul free?* I didn't know what to do with these realizations, so I went to a bookstore and found the shelves of spiritual self-help books, where I immersed myself. The resonance of their words retraced the palm lines on my hands in hopes of reminding me of what I had forgotten.

I went back to the hotel and talked to the Vastness. I knew there was something greater than me and since I didn't have an idea of what that was, I called it God. That day I began redefining the omnipresent for myself. The other God was Mama's God, but my God would be different. I was not yet versed in this area of my life but left for home on Sunday with new verve, ready to start anew and willing to be life's pupil.

Marlon was still annoyed with me, barely acknowledging my greeting when I arrived home. My children were ecstatic to see me and full of energy. I could equally match their energy because I was energized from doing things of interest to me. I felt empowered to continue spending time alone. I kept going to the hotel one weekend a month for several months. Marlon eventually came around and no longer fussed about my leaving.

I looked forward to the weekends by myself. In the quietude of the hotel, more questions surfaced. On my walks during my escape, I asked about the soul, my soul. *What is the essence of the Universe? What is my purpose?* The shield on the dome opened slightly, and a life beyond a white-collar job, a home, and two children winked at me, removing all skepticism about another possible existence. *Who am I?* I wondered.

At the hotel, I was more in tune with Kadian. She was that gleeful being who was in communication with our soul. She is the more evolved version of myself, helping me on my personal evolution. She is the interrupter on my life course, bringing awareness to challenge my current trajectory and helping Charm remember who she really is. And when I would leave the hotel, I embodied Charm again. She was the dominant version of myself. She viewed the world without an inner knowing. She was her family's modification, and now the world's puppet. Twenty-eight-year-old Charm meant to continue the pattern of fulfilling goals based on what she understood happiness to be.

You don't have to have a moniker to live two existences. I just happen to have one. As long as you are following the course society has been charting for you instead of your soul's course, then you are the protagonist and antagonist in your story. How does your antagonist try to reconnect with you? How does your protagonist resist, wanting to be the contrived heroine of a picture-perfect life?

With each passing day, I was enticed to make drastic changes. I had enough energy to begin climbing out of my crevice of sadness, enabling me to see the other choices that were available to me. No one else was aware of my sadness. And they weren't ready for the changes I was about to make because they were stuck in their own version of a charmed life and expected me to be happy living in mine. But I desperately wanted change.

I tested the waters with Marlon first. Our conversation topics at home were becoming limited to the children, and I wished for deeper communication between us. Marlon was uninterested in the horizon. He couldn't grasp the concepts I wanted to delve into. He couldn't understand why I wanted to go down this road. The beige house was all he yearned for.

Beyond home, I had no one around me who was ready for the conversations I wanted to have either. Some of my friends thought about a force larger than themselves, but they weren't willing to explore their inclinations. By 1996, I spent a copious amount of time in the self-help section of bookstores. I bought authors' cassette tapes to listen to in my car. At every opportunity, I read books and articles, I journaled, I imagined. This other life stood close by, enticing me to step right into it, my inner Kadian coaxing and encouraging me every step of the way.

Then, one morning, before Marlon left for work, I had a sudden urge to ask for a divorce.

He was stunned by my unexpected request. He cried, got on his knees, grabbed my hands, and begged me to stay. His response snapped me out of the vicarious life I had been entertaining. Unprepared for his reaction, I didn't know what to do. I couldn't look at him any longer. I removed my hands from his grip and backed away slowly. He got up, took his kerchief out of his back pocket, wiped his tears, and blew his nose. When Marlon left, I slid down the wall in the hallway and cried my eyes out with my back pressed against it.

Marlon kept calling me throughout the day asking why I wanted to do this to him. To the children. He wanted me to rethink my decision. That night while I readied Kamilah for bed, I pondered how much she loved her dad and the relationship they had. I asked myself, *How can I do this to her?* After putting Kamilah to bed, I walked into my son's room and sat on his car bed. Watching his chest rise and fall while he slept, I wallowed in selfishness. "He will need his father," I whispered. Kadian had become assertive, but she did not give me a plan for what came after. Charm was too afraid and lacked the understanding to follow through with a divorce. I didn't know how to proceed. My children were too important to me, and it scared me to break up their home.

That night, I let go of the new world I had discovered and began counting down the years until Khaleel graduated from high school. I took divorce off the table and continued on in Charm's reality. A reality I no longer wanted. I said nothing to Marlon of my decision to stay. "Sixteen years until Khaleel goes to college. I think I can do it," I muttered to myself.

A few days later, Marlon nervously asked if I was staying. I replied softly, "Yes," hoping Kadian wouldn't hear me. Marlon and I had no further discussion on the subject.

I stopped taking my monthly hotel breaks. This made Marlon happy. Kadian no longer had my attention, and the shield of the dome closed slowly and resealed itself. I focused on my children and their happiness to cope with my situation. I disregarded my own well-being to be Marlon's wife and Kamilah and Khaleel's mother. I withdrew. I resisted whenever Kadian attempted contact, and I suppressed the emotions that accompanied that resistance. I convinced myself this was the only way to go about waiting.

I gave up my newfound verve and fell back into my crevice of sadness once again. My life started losing its luster. The more I ignored my interests, the more discomfort reeked within, and the more I would lose energy. I was no longer available to anyone, not even to Charm. She, too, went silent since the vessel to carry out her storybook of happiness was now unavailable. I had to become numb to deal with my situation and stay married. Staying in my marriage and ignoring Kadian exacerbated my mental state and quelled my yearning for more. That charmed life was melting away to reveal the truth behind its veil. My picture-perfect life was stifling me.

After Khaleel was born, we decided not to extend our family. But as the saying goes, life doesn't always work out the way you plan it. I found myself pregnant again in 1997. I kept repeating to myself, *How am I going to survive this? I am stuck for another eighteen years in my marriage.*

The news of this pregnancy devastated me, and the sadness that sat at my bedside now overpowered me daily. Sadness was a part of my identity now, an appendage in my life. Watching my life with full awareness, I no longer wondered, "What can save me now?" but instead asked, "Who can save me now?"

To be honest, I didn't want this baby. I wanted her to go back. I didn't want her to be born to an unstable mother. But Kyra insisted on having me as a mother and arrived in November 1997. It was as if she knew I needed help. She was such a good baby. She hardly cried and slept a lot. But when she was awake and looked into my eyes, it felt as if she understood my fight. She had such a presence about her.

About six weeks after giving birth, the angst of not knowing who I really was came roaring back. I kept asking myself, "Who am I? Who is Kadian?" This was an incredibly stressful period for me. I felt like a mother whose child had been kidnapped at three years old and there was a possibility of never seeing that child again. A mother would always wonder about her child. Is he still alive? Is she safe? What does he look like now? While I constantly wondered about my lost child (me) and where she could be, I couldn't be the mother I wanted to be to my three children.

Life became even more difficult for me after giving birth to Kyra. My brain was fuzzy all the time, leaving me feeling unclear about many things. I did not have enough energy to work on matters to improve my state of being. My life came to a standstill, and I was descending into a deep depression. I didn't have the strength to accomplish daily tasks. I couldn't give my children what they needed. I began drinking a particular soda to get going physically. At first, I couldn't go a day without it. I drank it with every meal, then it became the first thing I drank in the mornings. Then, like shopping, it became addictive.

I felt inadequate as a mother and showed symptoms of clinical depression. I turned my thoughts to my children. I thought they were suffering. I felt they deserved a better mother. I didn't want them to end up depressed and unhappy in their lives like me. The unexpected news of my pregnancy, the pregnancy itself, giving birth, and postpartum depression forced me to my knees. I finally let go and surrendered in desperation. Only then I was able to see the hand of the Creator extended to me. I took hold of His hand.

His hand led me to find the courage to confide in a friend in the summer of 1998. I explained my sadness and finding it difficult to get out of bed each day. She understood my predicament because her sibling was going through depression. My friend took me to see a therapist. This therapist wasn't for me. We didn't connect.

I didn't give up. I tried a clinic near my home in the fall, where I was officially diagnosed with clinical depression. This clinic wasn't to my liking either. Their practice of medicating, a brief visit with a therapist, and written homework did not appeal to me. I wasn't able to do the written assignments. I was too depressed. After a few months, I stopped going to my appointments, and my hand slipped out of the Creator's grip. I postponed my search to cure my depression. My mental state worsened after that, and it became even more difficult for me to get out of bed.

I was alone in my struggle. Marlon turned a blind eye to my situation. It was difficult for him to face the fact that his wife was mentally ill. He handled my depression the way he handled all difficult situations. He ignored them until the situation resolved itself or was no longer an issue. Marlon didn't understand that he was ignoring his wife and her needs. He no longer asked how my day was because if he did, I would burst out crying. We did not talk about my depression. Marlon did what he thought could help me. He relieved me of the kids when he came home from work.

Marlon and I are products of the Jamaican culture. Depression is not a topic of discussion in a typical Jamaican household. It is not recognized as an illness by many people in the culture either. Jamaican women are strong mentally and physically. They use strength to deal with all circumstances. They find the strength every day to do their duties as a mother and a wife. That is how Mama, Grandma, Ms. Brown, and the rest of the women in my family dealt with unhappiness. I come from a strong, physical and mental stock of women. They find strength daily to accomplish what is expected of them, but I couldn't draw from their strength in this situation. Besides feeling inadequate as a mother, I also felt inadequate as a woman of my culture. I didn't have the will to get up every day, ignore my circumstance, and fulfill everyone else's needs. I felt weaker and mentally inferior to the women in my family and my culture, which added to my sadness.

I needed to be heard. I needed to be understood. When Marlon could not look at me, I turned in desperation to Ms. Brown. I picked up the phone and called her. After briefly listening to me, Ms. Brown took my cry for help as complaining. She said I should be grateful that I had a great husband, wonderful kids, and owned a home, with all the belongings most people would love to have. I wasn't surprised by her response. My pain has always been imperceptible to my mother. I got what I'd expected, but I had hoped for something different. I wasn't complaining about my life. I wanted to understand my sadness despite everything I had. Ms. Brown could not understand that material things and my family were not enough to get me out of bed anymore. Achieving material goods and succeeding at career goals can seem to others as if you're divinely favored or lucky and that should be enough. But it will never be enough.

I was devastated by her response because my hope for a different answer was so high. And yet, the truth is, I understood it. After that phone call with Ms. Brown, I remembered I was at the same crossroads where she stood when I was seven years old. My parents were not getting along when my brothers and I arrived in this country. Within a few months, Ms. Brown told us she was leaving our father. My brothers and I were shocked and in disbelief. We screamed, and we cried. Ms. Brown did not follow through with her decision and stayed in the marriage. She stayed for us. She was at the crossroads where a lot of women would stand, choosing their children over their own happiness. I too stood at that crossroads in 1996 and stayed for my children. So did my grandmother, aunts, cousins, and sisters. It was a pattern I could not eradicate. But the pattern was trying to eradicate itself because my desire to be authentically happy was too strong to ignore.

In 1999, I was taking care of Khaleel, a preschooler, and Kyra, a toddler, during the day. I was now crawling out of bed to bathe and feed them. To relieve myself from the crying, whining, and constant demands of me, I would put them in their car seats and drive around my neighborhood until they fell asleep. Sometimes it took ten minutes, sometimes thirty. Kamilah was now attending intermediate school, and I drove her around to her after-school activities. And when Marlon came home from work, I hurried to my downstairs office and worked on my projects for about four hours for Lucent Technologies. To be honest, I welcomed the relief from my children. I was now guzzling that soda for energy.

My condition continued to deteriorate with my busy schedule as emptiness ravaged my insides. I couldn't hold on any longer and finally succumbed to my intolerable sadness. I fell into depression's cold, dark room and sat there with my knees up and the door slightly ajar. I was disappearing, and all I could do was put my face between my knees and cry. I couldn't see a way out of this room. I did not have the energy, will, or strength to help myself. I was aware of my own decomposition yet unable to stop its decline.

One day, Khaleel wouldn't go to sleep during the car drive, so I drove back home and turned on his video game to keep him busy. Then I put Kyra in her crib, laid on my bedroom floor, and cried. I was unwell emotionally and physically. I called out to my son. He came running to my aid. I asked him if he knew how to dial the police on my cell phone.

He said, "Yes, Mom, 911," and he also showed me on the phone. It was a little past 11 a.m. I told him to check on me when the last two numbers turn fifteen to make sure I was awake. If I don't respond, I instructed him, call the police then. I gave him my cell phone. My son did exactly what I asked of him.

At 11:15 a.m. he shook me and asked in a soft, sweet but cautious voice, "Mommy, you okay?"

I said yes, then I showed him the next quarter hour.

After forty-five minutes of this routine, Khaleel laid down next to me, took my hand, and put it around himself, saying, "Don't be sad, Mommy. I'll stay with you." And he stayed with me until I was able to get up off my bedroom floor.

That day marked the lowest point of my life. I felt terrible enlisting my young son to help me through my crisis. I could not give up on being healthy. I had to get well for my children. The possibility of my children losing their mom to depression was now my greatest fear. This was a turning point in my life. If I didn't act now, I would ultimately disappear into depression's dark chamber with the door closed, never to be seen again. I was on my knees begging the Creator for help. This time I wouldn't let go of His hand.

With every ounce of energy I had left, I picked up the phone and dialed my friend. I felt guilty about burdening her with my issues, but my friend always listened to me with compassion. Understanding the urgency of that call, she phoned back by noon with a plan. She had spoken about my situation with the counselor at the school where she worked. The counselor said she had some information that could help me, and a meeting was set for the next day at my friend's house. I almost canceled, but it felt worse to let down my children and my friend, so I pushed myself to attend.

At my friend's house, it became clear in a matter of minutes that the counselor understood my circumstances. I left there hopeful and with more energy than when I arrived. That night before I fell asleep, I whispered over and over to myself, "Please help me" as I gripped the Creator's hand tighter. The next day, the counselor called with news. She had made an appointment for me to meet with a therapist she thought was a good fit for me. I went to the appointment.

I met a therapist who, after patiently listening to me, asked a question that would rattle my being. "Who do you have in your life you can turn to?" I burst into tears. I continued crying profusely during the session. My tears scoured my insides, cleansing years of sadness. Someone finally heard me.

I felt different from my biological family growing up. I didn't feel understood. I didn't feel understood in my marriage either. Marlon's idea of listening to me was him nodding while I talked and he watched television. My therapist wanted to know me. Not as the mother of Kamilah, Khaleel, and Kyra, or as Marlon's wife. She wanted to know Kadian Brown. What made Kadian Brown happy before she was a wife, mom, and computer developer? Through our sessions, she asked, "What does happiness look like for you?" My answer was symbolic. The purple house.

My children were brought into a couple of sessions. They were eleven, five, and two years old. It helped me understand how they felt and what it was like living with a mother like myself. Kamilah and Khaleel revealed they were afraid I was going to die. That was difficult for me to hear. Marlon also joined me in a few sessions at the therapist's request. He was informed about depression and mental illnesses. He learned in depth about my personal sadness and struggles. In the sessions, I expressed that I wanted him to really listen to me, get to know me, understand my needs. There was something deeper within me that I yearned for, and I wanted him to explore it with me.

Lingering in depression's room made it difficult for me to change course on my own. Working full-time at Lucent, trying to be a good mother to my three children, and being a wife overwhelmed and exhausted me every day. I was helpless and listless. I tried journaling as an outlet to express my sadness, but my malignant state made it difficult to write. At times I would only jot down a word or a sentence. I would write *weak* or *lost* once, then be done for the day. When I was able to, I penned a page full of one word—*lost, lost, lost, lost*—or write a couple of pages about my feelings. Every entry breathed life back into my body.

An excerpt from my journal on June 14, 1999, reveals what it was like being in depression's cold, dark room:

> *I am trying to evaluate what's happening to me on my own, but everything is so confusing. My brain and my thoughts are not functioning as normal... I am unable to concentrate or think for very long. My memory gets worse on a daily basis... I feel unintelligent. I have no confidence or self-esteem anymore. I am dying slowly. It is hard to grasp what's happening to me. I AM LOST. I am living unconsciously. I am unable to feel. I have No Spirit! God, why me?*

Being able to set goals again and move in the direction of action from where I stood was somewhat difficult but not impossible. I needed an external force to help me, and I found that external force in my children. They were my motivation.

Beside journaling, therapy skyrocketed my healing. My energy improved and gave me the mental capacity to make better decisions. Setting goals and feeling successful again wasn't authentic happiness, but I would be moving in the right direction instead of in a downward spiral.

I learned you must find anything to motivate you while sitting in depression's room. Who is in your corner? What can create positive movement in your life? What can you strive for here? Any action will keep depression from swallowing you whole and disappearing you into its darkness. Then, when motivated enough, you will have enough strength and courage to walk out of its stronghold onto the journey to free your soul.

CHAPTER SIX

Escaping Depression's Cold, Dark Room

I felt like I was starting anew in a somewhat unwilted place. My therapist's positive disposition and professionalism without criticism or judgment helped me to function in the world again. I felt safe with her to express my desires. Things at home were improving slowly, getting better nonetheless.

Marlon tried to make me happy. The therapist told him that whenever I wanted to talk to turn the television off, and he did at first. He at least tried to seem interested in what I had to say. We read books together, had some conversations that I wanted to have, and I was being more honest about my feelings. Marlon did anything I asked because he loved me. My quality of life improved, and I was able to lift my head to see the streak of light entering depression's room. The light represented hope of leaving its confinement one day.

It wasn't long before it became difficult for Marlon to keep up with the intensity of making me happy. His attention became spurious and sporadic, and he eventually reverted to his old ways. I realized it was not his job to make me happy. This was my work. I was determined to heal myself, so I relieved him of that responsibility. I never invited him on my hunt for authentic happiness again and decided to continue without him.

Even though I'd had some progress in therapy, I refused anti-depressants. My therapist thought an alternative way of healing would help move my depression along. I knew a few people who relied on anti-depressants to live. I wanted to eradicate depression altogether. I agreed to try her suggestion. She introduced me to one of the most unselfish, dedicated, and incredible souls I've ever met: chiropractor Dr. Harry Schick. After my first visit with Dr. Schick, I left his office extremely tired. I slept for over ten hours after arriving home. I don't think I'd ever slept that long. I woke up the next day refreshed and revitalized. My mental health was the clearest it had been in about two years. I cleaned my house, cooked, and took care of my children while working from home. I learned about alternative ways to heal the body without medicine, about organic foods, and developed healthier eating habits I incorporated into my life and my family's life over the coming years.

With Dr. Schick's help, my mental and physical state improved rapidly. Every day, it got easier to get out of bed, take care of myself, home, children, and work at my corporate job. I finally stood up and followed the streak of light right out of depression's room thanks to therapy and alternative healing. I was free, and no longer lingered in its darkness, but was wholly aware of my susceptibility to its reach.

Being free breathed life back into Charm. I resumed implementing goals for happiness from her perspective. Charm's perception of happiness was preferable to feeling stuck and powerless. I understood where that would lead if I did nothing to stop my descent. I would never allow that to happen to me again. The feelings of emptiness and being lost weren't gone, but I was glad to have those feelings once more rather than the complete numbness of depression. Besides, an awakened Charm could possibly become an instrument of Kadian's requests one day. I embraced my undesirable reality with a new awareness: I made the choice at the crossroads, therefore I have the power to choose differently.

I continued seeing Dr. Schick three days a week for over a year. He was instrumental in helping me turn my life around

with spinal manipulation, NAET (allergy elimination tech-
niques), and other holistic therapies. My children and I have
since formed a lasting relationship with him, and he is still our
doctor today.

I had to keep Charm's light burning for now. Charm wasn't my
desired state of being but she gave me energy to direct my life. I
didn't want to be physically and mentally slumbering because that
would lead to inescapable depression. I promised myself that if I
ever felt like I was slipping away again, then I'd change course and
follow what makes me happy. So, I continued setting goals—
succeeding or failing was inconsequential.

In the fall of 2000, I ecstatically accepted an opportunity to buy
and manage a nursing agency in Mount Vernon, New York. I
didn't question whether this new venture would make me happy
or purposeful. I just loved being motivated again. Trying a different
career was stimulating after being dissatisfied in my corporate job
for years. I dove into rebuilding my agency, which had one
employee when I bought it, as the rest had resigned because of the
previous owner. By 2002, I grew my agency to sixty people
consisting of full-time and part-time employees, contractors, and
seasonal workers.

With some degree of contentment in my life and depression
resting, I heard that strange tone again, the one that contacted me
in my car in the parking lot during lunch hour. Its visitations were
comforting though sporadic, faint, and brief.

One morning driving into work, I picked up on its communication and felt tingling in my hands and feet. I was sensing different
forms of transmission simultaneously. I pulled over to the side of
the road, turned off the engine, and allowed the tone to penetrate
my being. My busy life slowly drifted away as the tone fused with
my molecules, creating arrhythmic notes that felt like my own. I
named it my unique tone. I was floating in a fluid space that felt
eerily familiar. My beach-breeze experience was contacting me in a

different car—my car this time. Whatever was impressed upon me as a child revealed itself again.

I was being urged to remember that a greater life awaited me. I felt my existence being repurposed in this altered state. *That was God's infinite, harmonious system,* I thought when it passed. I tried to pin down my unique tone's visits to a particular time, space, or moment, but I couldn't. I anxiously awaited its next contact.

Even though I had successfully resurrected my agency, I became disinterested in it after some time. This familiar outcome after a successful goal didn't unnerve me. After all, I was in the recurring theme of a materialistic life. A life I knew all too well. It was still in a better place than clinical depression. Charm continued working on her version of happiness and gave me another goal to carry out. In 2002, I bought my first retail store, Prominent Fashions, in Mount Vernon, New York. I worked there during the day, and at night I did the scheduling for my agency at home.

I needed help in my store and since Ms. Brown lived close by, I asked her to work with me. This was the first time we would spend a great deal of time together since I moved out in 1991. Immediately, we had problems between us. Ms. Brown hadn't changed. She didn't agree with the way I conducted business and wanted to control everything. We argued incessantly. I was falling back into the dysfunctional environment I had moved away from and soon bemoaned asking her for assistance. Despite everything, my businesses flourished.

My mental health continued improving. I wasn't free of depression. I sensed it hovering, waiting for an opportunity to arrest me at any moment, but I could manage it. My home life improved, and my family and I were vacationing again. Marlon and I enjoyed our children excelling in school, their extra-curricular activities, and winning sport competitions. We had a plenitude of gifts under the Christmas tree and the material belongings many people would want. Unhappiness began spreading like invasive weeds with every materialistic goal I achieved. A hunger for something greater gnawed at my insides. I was approaching the crossroads again. I knew I needed to resume the search for my missing inner child, but I ignored my hunger by keeping busy while keeping a close eye on those weeds. I had to finish raising my children.

It was becoming difficult to drive into New York every day. I couldn't be at home for my children. They were getting older and involved in many activities, and it was necessary to be accessible to them. Besides, I wanted to be away from my store. I had no passion for it. I wanted to be away from Ms. Brown. It was becoming increasingly difficult to be around her. I decided to continue paying her to manage the day-to-day operations of Prominent Fashions while I took care of everything else and only visited the store on occasion.

I had gone from almost disappearing to being content. That was a huge gain, but my deep desires were like a sleeping volcano. They had gone dormant during my depression, but were bubbling up and becoming active again. My desires grew more compelling with greater awareness and presence in my life. I noticed I was only surviving in Charm's reality but not thriving. *Who am I?* I wondered. I missed the allure of the horizon. *What is my purpose?* I often thought to myself. I wanted to be in conversations with Kadian again. I missed her whispers. I noticed she wasn't antagonizing me with questions to make me take pause.

On the morning of November 25, 2002, Ms. Brown called to tell me that Brian was murdered in Jamaica. She received the news from my father. I didn't know what to do, so after talking a few minutes, I told her I'd call her back. Feeling almost paralyzed by the death of my baby brother, I called Marlon to let him know, hoping he would come home. He was five minutes away at the train station, but he did not.

He said, "Sorry to hear about your brother. We'll talk later," and then he went to work.

I sat on my bedroom floor and cried. I couldn't get up to take Khaleel and Kyra to school. It's difficult to put into words how the news about my brother hit me that morning, but years later Khaleel and I had a conversation about poignant moments in a person's life that are seared onto our memory. The morning I told him Uncle Brian died was number one on his list.

"I was playing my video game as usual that morning, waiting for you," Khaleel said. "But you hadn't shouted down the stairs yet to let me know when it was time to leave for school. I noticed that I had defeated more bosses in my game than usual and began to wonder what you were doing because Kyra and I were going to be late. So, I climbed the stairs and walked down the hall to your bedroom. I found you on the floor crying, and I had never seen you cry before. That in itself was shocking, and I just stood there feeling helpless. But that's not what stunned me. I was taken aback by the profound look of sadness on your face that right now, in this moment, I can still see.

"Then you looked up to see me standing there, wiped your face, and said, 'Uncle Brian died.'

"I didn't really know my uncle, so the news really didn't upset me that much when you said it. But what affected me most of all was your sadness and feeling helpless to soothe your pain."

Khaleel continued, "Whenever I see a woman that's important to me cry, it brings me back to that moment of you crying on your bedroom floor, and then I feel helpless all over again. I just want to help them get through their situation because of how the most important woman in my life felt that day."

After returning home from taking Khaleel and Kyra to school, I called Ms. Brown back and spoke to her briefly. A sudden tiredness came over me, and I fell asleep. When I woke up, I drove to Philadelphia to see my father. Even though my father and I didn't speak often, I wanted to be there for him. I wasn't thinking about the night he threw me out in 1984 or his mistreatment of me.

I could only envision a father who had just lost his son. Brian was his favorite child, and his death would devastate my father. My father was shocked when he opened his front door and saw me standing there. After spending a few hours with him, I drove to Hartsdale, New York, to see Ms. Brown. I couldn't imagine her pain. I didn't care about the state of our relationship. I only saw a mother who just lost her child. I stayed with her for the next few days.

Two weeks later, my children, Ms. Brown, and I flew to Jamaica for Brian's funeral. My father went separately, and Marlon arrived a few days after. I put aside the burden of Brian's death to be strong for my parents. Ms. Brown had mentally checked out, so my father and I took care of most of the arrangements. My father tried to be strong, but his hands shook and his voice quivered.

The first night in Jamaica, my daughters slept in one bed with my mother and my son slept in the other bed with my father. I sat in a chair in the bedroom watching them sleep, ignoring my tired body. Staring at them, I thought a lot about my relationship with my parents. The last time I was in the same room with them was in 1984 during the worst turmoil of my life. I now sat in the same room with them during their worst turmoil. I wanted to forgive my parents for the past, but forgiveness isn't instantaneous. Forgiveness is a process, and this wasn't the time to mull over what I wanted. I just wanted to be there for them and to ease their pain. I headed downstairs when I heard wailing.

I opened the balcony door to witness Adrian and silence in competition with each other. Silence wanted to remain its obscure, amorphous, soundless self. But Adrian's intense grief was intrusive, threatening to give shape and sound to the silence. I sat amid them, held Adrian's hand, and looked at the moon. Adrian's weeping filled the villa as silence fought against being defined. I didn't say anything. I didn't cry. I just sat still with my gaze frozen on the night sky. Silence was almost becoming form when Adrian grew tired and went to bed. It was able to hang on to its mystical, unseeable self. Silence won by default. I remained in the dark.

Quiet and still, I yearned for the presence of my unique tone. I understood now this was not something I could summon; it summoned me. It did not in that early morning.

After Brian's funeral, Marlon and I took the children to a beach in Ocho Rios. It was Kamilah's birthday, and I wanted the children to have a little fun in spite of this family tragedy. Even though we were in Jamaica due to an unfortunate circumstance, it was a break from our regular, busy life of work, school, and routines. I laid on my beach towel in the sand spying on my family through my sunglasses, enjoying this break from their normal lives.

I giggled as the whitecaps' cold tips nipped at Kyra's heels and sent her skipping back on to the sand. I chuckled at Kamilah besting her uncle Adrian in a swimming match and him asking for a rematch. "She's a pool swimmer, that's why!" was his excuse after his second loss. Khaleel found a friend around his age, and they built castles. Khaleel filled his bucket with sand, turned it over, then patted his fortress into shape.

Pictures of my life flashed before me as Khaleel's worker-bee hands shaped his fortress. First pat, I'm lost in this beautiful, perfect scene. Third pat, I reflect on my nursing agency. Pat again, I see the smile on Kamilah's face as she bettered her uncle. Pat, pat, envisioning the life I'm going back to with sadness. Pat, pat, pat, Kyra twirling in the sand from right to left and back, now looking like a churro rolled in cinnamon. *Lord, I have to wash her hair later.* Pat, pat, pat, thoughts of my life back home.

I blinked away from Khaleel's busy hands and looked out at the sea and the horizon. This picturesque view sprinkled tracings of happiness in my dissatisfied life that would later gnaw at me constantly. I didn't wonder about death. I wondered about happiness and if we'd ever meet.

My desires bubbled intently within, not to a point of eruption yet, but enough to feel uncomfortable. I decided right then to dissolve my nursing agency within the New Year when I got back home. My verve for it had long passed.

We arrived home just before the last weekend of 2002. I couldn't withstand the weight Brian's death had on me any longer. My emotions demanded solitude to settle down, so I packed a small bag and drove to the nearest hotel to escape for the weekend. I told Marlon that I wouldn't be answering my phone and to call only in case of an emergency. "If anyone calls for me, don't give away details of my escape. I'll call back at my earliest convenience."

After checking in at the hotel, I tottered to my room, not realizing my legs had stepped back from their supportive role. I opened the door, feebly wobbled a few feet in, and put my travel bag down as I could not go any further. My purse fell to the floor and the door closing behind me was the last thing I heard. Everything went blurry, and my life froze in time, awaiting my presence to it again. The last month came crashing down on me without me seeing it coming. I woke up on the floor moments later. I had collapsed.

I awakened to the room slightly spinning. Somewhat confused by what had just happened, I dragged myself to the nearby chair to regain my composure. Minutes later, I walked unsteadily to the bed and laid on my back. Tears leaked slowly at first then flooded down my face. I hadn't really grieved my brother's death. Grief oozed out when Ms. Brown told me the news and I cried briefly. Grief oozed out when I went to the store to buy Brian's suit alone. Again grief oozed out when I went to the morgue in Jamaica to view his body. Then again when his casket laid on our paternal grandfather's verandah. But here in the hotel, grief gushed out of me as if I had finally given it permission to show itself. I couldn't contain it any longer. I wept the way Adrian wept on the balcony in Jamaica.

I remembered how close I was to my twin brothers when we were growing up. I remembered seeing them on the train platform soon after my father threw me out. Brian had shouted my name from across the platform to get my attention. I'd run upstairs to meet them, and Brian had sped towards me, shouting, "My sister, my sister, I love you." And I remembered him picking me up and spinning me around.

When my father walked out on Ms. Brown and my brothers' life, I had gone to see them. I remembered how my brothers had bawled. Even though they were sixteen years old, I laid in the bed between Adrian and Brian and stayed with them while they cried. They were like babies again.

Over the years, I thought my brothers turned to drugs because my father left them. I hadn't realized their lives also changed the night my father threw me out. All our lives changed that night. We each dealt with the situation differently. I was free and took control of my life, while my brothers couldn't cope and turned to drugs. If I had returned home after my father threw me out, I wondered, could I have saved them from a life of drug addiction? I felt responsible for what had happened to my twin brothers and wished their lives had turned out differently.

My father blamed himself for Brian's death. He didn't want to live after Brian's departure from this world. I didn't know how else to help my father other than having more frequent conversations. He now understood the significance of the night he'd made me leave and the decision to abandon his sons. I had to let go of wanting to save them all and welcomed the revelation of not being responsible for anyone's reality but my own.

I remembered Adrian and Brian sitting in the kid's floater pool with Kamilah when she was a year old and splashing her with water. I remembered Brian taking Kamilah to the park and pushing her on the swings. Brian was the fun brother, the fun uncle, the fun everything. I wept until my stomach hurt. I wept because I'd said mean things to him over the years. I wished I was more understanding of what he had to endure. I wept because my beautiful brother died a drug addict and never found himself again. My brother died unhappy and lost.

After Brian's funeral in Jamaica, an elderly lady had come up to me and introduced herself. She had known my brother well. She said Brian wanted to die. He felt he had nothing to live for and life wasn't worth living anymore. She had tried many times to talk him out of wrongdoings, but he never listened. My brother was shackled by insufferable hopelessness and disappeared into depression's room with the door welded shut. It was as if Brian deemed the crevasse between who he was destined to be and where he was in his life too great for him to overcome. I remembered when I sat in depression's room with the door ajar, feeling the separation between the modified me and my soul. The will and exertion it took for me to actually escape seemed almost impossible at the time. *Where would he even begin at that level of hopelessness?* I could imagine my brother's despondency at the mountainous climb ahead of him.

Brian was a gifted athlete. He had wanted to play professional baseball. He was also a genius in math and loved science. My brothers would've been great engineers. They could fix anything. As children, they used to take everything apart to see how the mechanism worked, then put it back together. Brian was loving and compassionate. He had a penchant for bringing home strays. Once, he brought home a rabbit he found, which he named Playboy, and gave it to me as a gift. Brian found two stray cats, which he gave to Ms. Brown. My cousins named them Princess and Sabrina. He brought home a few stray dogs and hid them in the basement from Ms. Brown. Brian was funny and charming. He could make a room of people laugh. All that greatness wrapped up inside of him and he couldn't stand in it. Death was easier than freeing his soul, it might have seemed to him.

The night before we left Jamaica, I watched as Adrian sunk deeper into unhappiness and further separated from who he was supposed to be in this life. I worried he would suffer the same fate as Brian. *Could his twin's death motivate him enough to pursue authentic happiness?* The night before our departure, Adrian cried an ocean of tears. His immediate family leaving him and being separated by a body of water sent him into a state of anxiety and panic. Worry was evident in my parents' eyes as their spirits were being tortured by their own painful thoughts and guilt. I didn't know how to help them or Adrian. I can't help someone find happiness and peace if I haven't found mine. All I could do was choose to stay positive and hopeful for everyone.

Brian had called me to wish me a happy Mother's Day in 2002. He told me he loved me. He wished he was different and that our relationship was like when we were kids. He said, "Charm, you were my mom growing up. You took care of me. When you weren't in the house anymore, everything changed." And we both cried. It would be the last time we spoke before his death.

I eventually fell asleep and awoke at 7:30 a.m. I took a shower, made tea, and lingered in the sitting area of my hotel room, overcome with sadness. I wanted to go downstairs to the hotel's lobby for breakfast, but I didn't have the energy to dress myself. It was almost twenty-four hours since I'd had a meal. Calling for room service seemed an arduous chore, and I dragged myself back to bed and burst into tears. I had so much I wanted to say to Brian and wished he were alive for me to do so.

The hotel phone rang in the middle of my contemplation, startling me. When I answered it, Ms. Brown said apprehensively, "Marlon told me you went away for the weekend to be alone." She was worried and wanted to make sure I was okay. I assured her that it was only a brief mental and emotional break and I'd call her back on Monday. We hung up, and I laid back down. Minutes later, the hotel phone rang again; it was my father. He too was worried and wanted to check on me. I was furious with Marlon.

The goal in therapy was to stay married and find happiness within our dynamic. Marlon learned how to make me happy, and I had made peace with the promises he had broken, for authentic happiness was a journey I wanted to explore. Not him. He disregarded other areas of our marriage, too, such as my well-being.

I was furious because Marlon never listened to me. He didn't protect me. He was not there for me when I was at my weakest.

My therapist's question came back to me from our first session together. "Who do you have in your life you can turn to?" It was on repeat in my head. I had been the driver of the car that was our marriage. Over the years, I needed help with the driving, but Marlon never took the wheel. I wanted him to drive, especially when I was weak, vulnerable, or tired. More often, I wanted him to take the initiative and drive, or just share the driving with me. I was tired of doing the driving all by myself.

Marlon didn't help me during the worst tragedy in my life. When I called him to tell him that my brother died that morning, he was only five minutes away yet he didn't come home to console me. He didn't call me during the day. He called me when he got home from work after he had settled in. He didn't help me with booking our flights, hotel, and car arrangements for Jamaica, or any arrangement at all. Now, he couldn't do the one thing I had asked of him during this terrible ordeal: "Don't tell anyone where I am." I needed him to drive the car because I was tired and weak. Who do I have in my life to turn to? I had no one. Not even my husband.

My remembrances went from Brian to why I wanted to divorce Marlon. I wrote pages of memories in my mind of all the reasons for my dissatisfaction in our marriage. When I wrote all I remembered, the mental pages swirled slowly around my head as I revisited each one. My anger escalated, and the pages twirled and rocked side to side like a metallic pinwheel caught up in a passing squall. The angrier I became, the faster the pages spun. I was no longer crying because of Brian's death; I cried because I was tired of driving the damn car through the storms of our marriage alone.

After that, I slept for most of the day. I ordered room service for dinner, but by the time it arrived, I had lost my appetite. I thought about Brian and how he died an unhappy human being. This frightened me. I knew I would end up dying unhappily like my brother if I didn't make a change, but change frightened me. I ate half of my burger to avoid thinking about the actuality of life. I drank some water and went back to sleep.

I slept until it was almost time to check out. I dressed as quickly as I could and left the hotel.

I wasn't ready to reenter Charm's suffocating snow globe, so I drove to a park near my home and sat in my car. I asked Brian for forgiveness. I talked to God. I thought about my marriage some more. Divorce panicked me still. I was afraid to create the life bursting inside of me because I chose my children's happiness at the crossroads and ignored my own. I didn't know how to give them what they needed *and* locate my happiness. *Would I be a terrible mother if I chose myself sometimes?* I felt limited to my accomplishments and my obsession to not be a mother like Ms. Brown. Yet, I couldn't stop thinking about the greater me percolating within. A version I knew existed, but I wasn't being. I didn't know how to do both. *How can I begin to feel free?* With the original question still on my mind—*Who is Kadian?*—a new question was being born: *Where is she?* These were my "questions that have no right to go away." All my wondering ignited communications with Kadian again and I embraced it. I wouldn't ignore her whispers anymore.

When I arrived home, I did not speak to Marlon. I was still furious. Being back at home, I couldn't deny my overwhelming dissatisfaction with my life. I took steps immediately to dissolve my agency. I kept Prominent Fashions for financial reasons only and dissolved my agency in 2003. I felt unmotivated in the New Year. I wasn't disillusioned about what the end result of that feeling would be. I knew it was the slow route to clinical depression and ultimately slipping into its room. I did not want to revisit clinical depression and tried to get ahead of it.

This time, I confided in a good friend before I lost control of my life again. She suggested that I attend church. "You will find answers there," she said. Charm agreed. I began attending my grandmother and mother's place of worship in early 2003 for answers. It soon became another tool to stave off my depression until I could make a commitment to my soul.

My biological family is of the Christian faith, but attending church wasn't a big part of our lives growing up. We went on Easter Sundays only until I was about ten years old. The other times were for weddings or baptisms. When I walked into the church in 2003, the choir was singing Mama's favorite hymn, "Blessed Assurance." I felt it was a sign, and my eyes filled with tears of happiness. I really enjoyed it there at first. I remembered Mama singing certain hymns. I was learning the Bible in depth, and I was happy about that. I assisted in the bookstore. The bookstore wasn't thriving, so I worked very closely with the person in charge to make it flourish. It was like managing my retail establishment. I realized I love the thrill of making something almost lifeless come back to life, like rebuilding my agency.

I forced my children and Marlon to join with me, something I would later regret. My girls were in the choir, and all three kids were involved in many of the ministries for children and young people. In church, Charm continued reading from her storybook of happiness that encouraged the idea of Marlon and I growing old together. It reminded me of our dream of buying an RV when we retired to travel around the country. *Whose dream is that?* I knew that was Kadian asking. *Not mine*, I whispered back.

I could sense my sadness along with my smallness when I considered Charm's storybook of happiness. I was creating her dream every time I engaged with church. She felt satisfied after every successful goal. Even though her dream scared me, I felt my children needed me for now, and I went along with her plans knowing I still had the power to change my mind. I settled into this life and continued to delay my search for authentic happiness.

I stopped going to therapy shortly after joining church. It had taken me as far as it could, and I was grateful for our sessions.

I was confident that I could manage my life on my own without becoming clinically depressed again. I learned ways to keep depression at bay. I took walks when my low state nudged me. I journaled my feelings. I talked to my God often. I asked God to not give up on me, for I hadn't forgotten about my personal happiness, I just had it on pause. I also had my own unique tone that showed up for me now and again. And with Kadian reminding me of what thrilled me inside, I felt secure enough to stick with the decision I made at the crossroads for now.

By the end of 2003, life became mundane and routine. Unmotivating. No spontaneity. Nothing new to accomplish. These are the moments to pay close attention to. I had a sudden awareness about my life. I realized I was existing but no longer creating anything new. There was no lure. Charm's storybook had disappeared into the vastness, like the vision of growing old with Marlon. She had gone dormant because she was unable to motivate me. I was stagnant again. I recognize the space I was in. I was back to coping. Kadian was constantly reminding me of the life that awaited me. I busied myself to drown out her voice. *Soon,* I would say to her. *Soon.* I had to be cautious as my walks and journaling weren't sustaining me as much. I knew I was treading on a dangerous path. My sadness was growing again. I couldn't sustain the busyness that was keeping depression at bay.

Nothing seemed to be working to keep my low states from coming on. And they were occurring more often. The unhappy part of me blared and demanded an immediate response while Kadian stood glaring, daring me not to. I couldn't look away any longer. I gave my authentic feelings some attention one morning, and a barrage of sadness hit me and wouldn't stop firing. With trepidation, I sat with it and came face to face with clinical depression for the second time. I had sunk to one of my lowest states in a very long time. I felt how unhappy I was with my marriage, business, physical appearance, and overall life. I realized that to cope in Charm's reality in my twenties, I had numbed myself. I stood at depression's door once again, but refused to enter. No way was I going back in there.

Instead, I turned away and launched a spiritual life that many people in my life were unaware of. I cloistered myself in its silence and meditated on the horizon. I immersed myself in my spiritual/self-help books. I listened to the CD versions of the books at every opportunity. When my family fell asleep at nights, I crawled out of bed and sauntered towards the sound of silence into my living room. In this space, I held many conversations with God. I practiced silencing my mind, hoping to interpret its chatter. Sometimes I sat in the linen closet in my bathroom. Mostly, I cried there. Those were the nights I felt the enormous gap between the modified me and my soul. I often thought of Brian and how he might have felt about his life. I wanted to rediscover who I was. I knew he would want that for me.

In February 2004, I procured my biggest step on this new path by attending a spiritual retreat about the soul in San Francisco. I didn't hesitate when I saw it online or that it was far away. It seemed similar to escaping to the hotel on the weekends to work on my personal happiness. Except this respite would include going three thousand miles away to listen to a spiritual teacher's explanation on soul matters. This choice hadn't come from an outward observation of happiness but from an inner stirring. I've had these rare occurrences before—when something feels so incredibly right or wrong that it shifts your core. The extraordinary encounters of brushing up against inspiration.

I visited San Francisco for five days. Marlon was a good father, so I didn't have to worry about the children. I attended the retreat for two and a half days and I explored San Francisco on foot on the other days. The solitude gave me time to think, practice the exercises from the retreat, and journal. I conversed with God for a long time in the mornings and at night.

Upon returning home from my escape, I took online spiritual and self-help classes to continue my learning of the soul and intuition. I did research via the internet. I continued engaging with

Kadian and the part of me that desired to be authentically happy. My secret life of spiritual growth revived me, and depression was out of reach once again.

The commitment to my spiritual growth gave me a new belief. I could raise my children *and* tend to my own happiness. I had adopted a new perspective with Kadian's help. I promised to never ignore that part of me again and committed to my spiritual growth. I vowed never to stop searching for authentic happiness.

CHAPTER SEVEN
Unhealthy Unloading

My secret spiritual life calmed me. I'd been on edge since I landed in this country so I embraced all the peace I could attain. This period of peace was preparing me for the biggest catalyst looming in my life. Something that would disrupt my inner being and frazzle my core.

In September 2005, my mother called me with disturbing news. My landlord wanted to terminate my lease immediately. Trying to unearth this situation and comprehend the reasoning behind it was not easy. Ms. Brown wasn't being cooperative, so we fought every day. As it turned out, Ms. Brown had put my store in grave financial disaster from the time I allowed her to manage Prominent Fashions. I discovered that she hid many things from me. It was difficult to engage with her on my terms. She triggered the rage inside of Charm, and my private rituals weren't enough to regain my peace. I was falling back into generational patterns in the way my family handled conflict.

While processing the disturbances, I felt the pressure of going through them. I had to go beyond being aware of the problem to not succumbing to Ms. Brown's dominance and control. I didn't know it yet, but I was being called to a greater potential. This would require facing the past, undoing my modification, and

merging my inner protagonist and antagonist to produce a singu-
lar, greater me. To undo my modification, I needed to find a
healthy way to unload (how we express discomfort), eradicate
patterns, and dismantle outdated beliefs—these steps were perti-
nent to becoming that greater self.

It wouldn't be easy, and I understood after undergoing this
process why most people steer clear of such attempts and continue
on a course of inauthentic happiness. This new resolve took me on
the most painful journey of my existence since falling into depression's room. I had to walk consciously, honestly, and courageously
to take Kadian's hand. The overwhelming feeling scared me. I
didn't know anyone who else was doing this excavating of their life
to confide in or lean on for support. There were times that I
wanted to hide behind depression's door again. It felt easier to
do so.

Standing up to Ms. Brown and removing her control proved
difficult, almost impossible, but I had to free my soul from its
confinements to live the life I wanted to live. I no longer wanted to
succumb to society's plans and other people's expectations of me. I
proceeded cautiously while fighting with the world's view of
happiness.

Ms. Brown and I were in our own personal battle for control of
my life. She had given up control of hers to Grandma and wanted
to control mine. And I had given her more control of it than I was
conscious of. Patterns were showing everywhere. The difference
between Ms. Brown and me was that I wanted my power back, all
of it and I was willing to fight for it. I knew this would not be an
easy feat, for she had had control since I was six years old, but I
was ready to fight for Kadian. When a desire is so strong, all the
infinitesimal molecules of the Universe will come together to
present opportunities to work on the issue. It won't solve the situation but will bring together all the components necessary to choose
a greater you.

Why did Ms. Brown and I bicker over *my* stores and who was
really in charge? I had bought Prominent Fashions, including the

inventory stock, fixtures, and all accounts, from my landlord, who owned the building where my nursing agency was located. When my landlord wanted to retire from retail to go into wholesale, he had approached me with a proposition. He said he would teach me everything about the retail and wholesale business and stay with me until I was comfortable without him. I had become disinterested with my agency and wanted to try something different, so I said yes. This man had asked me to promise him one thing before we signed on the dotted line. He asked me to not allow Ms. Brown to manage the business.

"I know you live far away and will be inclined to have your mother help you out. But your mother has been shopping in my store for over a decade, and her spendthrift ways and lack of business knowledge would run the business into the ground. Hire a real manager when that time comes."

I broke that promise when I put Ms. Brown in charge of the daily operations of Prominent Fashions from 2003 to September 2005. It had become difficult to drive to New York from New Jersey every day, manage my own store, tend to my three children, work a corporate job, and manage my nursing agency, all while being depressed. I didn't have enough energy to give my store the attention it required, so, I let her manage it. This further tightened the grip of control she had over my life.

Ms. Brown didn't listen to any of my solutions or instructions. And since I wasn't present to the daily workings of the business, she did whatever she wanted to. She paid her personal finances with the daily cash so I wouldn't see it on the credit card receipts. In my absence, Ms. Brown neglected the expenses of the store and mismanaged the inventory. Prominent Fashions fell into financial difficulty partly because she gave merchandise to customers on consignment, allowing them to pay whenever they wanted, and even to take merchandise without paying off previous balances. There were many times she didn't log the transaction or remember that the merchandise was taken. It got out of control, and I never collected on some of the outstanding balances. This situation was not entirely her fault, and I took accountability for my absence.

Ms. Brown felt that we were in some kind of partnership because the landlord was her friend and I had allowed her to manage my store for almost three years with little interference from me. Let's be clear, I paid for everything with my own money, all documents were signed by me, the landlord trained only me, and he communicated with only me until he trusted that I could manage on my own. Since I wasn't visible in my own business, customers and family members thought she owned Prominent Fashions, and she didn't correct anyone. When I found out, I did not correct anyone either. I am not hung up on small details, and that seemed a small detail to me.

The landlord did not want to revisit the terms of the lease because I had broken our trust. I expected as much, and I didn't blame him either. He gave me until the end of the year to move out. I wasn't having much luck finding a new place that could hold the amount of merchandise I had. In January 2006, I had to settle for a small, temporary space and put most of the merchandise in storage. So, for my move, I asked a few of our church members for a helping hand, which they graciously extended. The landlord asked me to abide by specific instructions as part of the agreement for early termination of my lease. While packing, Ms. Brown began breaking all the instructions in the agreement. Every time I reminded her of what I signed my name to, she argued with me. She made her insolence known the more our disagreement escalated.

Ms. Brown has a different persona with her church members, so it confounded me when the real Ms. Brown showed up in the church members' view. They said nothing about the ensuing argument at first, but their furrowed brows, squinted eyes, and slight gaping of their mouths expressed their bewilderment.

As our disagreement continued escalating, one of the women turned to Ms. Brown and said, "Why are you talking to your daughter this way? Isn't there a better way to address this situation?"

Seeming embarrassed, Ms. Brown calmed down and changed her tone. The interruption broke up our argument, and I quietly seethed. I was tired of her unceasing contempt and stormed out in a state of distress and pity for myself.

"Why do I have a mother like this?" I shouted in the air while opening my car door. I got in and slammed the door. Tears rolled down my face as I drove off. I couldn't stop crying so I pulled into the church parking lot to compose myself.

At that exact moment my cell phone rang. My friend heard the distress in my voice when I answered and asked, "What is the matter?"

I unloaded on my friend. I felt safe enough to do so. She gave me the space and time to speak about the argument. My friend listened with kindness and without judgment, as I continued crying and unloading. When I finished spewing, she said, "You must look at this differently."

"How?" I shouted.

"Your mother taught you, and is still teaching you, what kind of mother *not* to be. I have seen you with your children, and the relationships are not the same."

This incontrovertible truth flung my car door open and shook sense into me. That validation of my motherhood quickly dispelled that old pattern of bad mothering in my family and soothed my spirit. I indeed had a different relationship with my children because I strived every day to live up to my definition of mom. Sometimes, awareness comes when a person says or does something to shift one's perspective. My friend observed the veritable truth of a pattern I had started dismantling as a child.

Until then, I'd only discussed my relationship with Ms. Brown in depth with my therapist. I didn't even discuss my true feelings with Marlon. Every day I wished I had a different relationship with her; some days, I wished she wasn't my mother at all.

· · ·

I moved into a permanent retail space in June 2006, convincing myself that I should keep Ms. Brown on as an employee to help her financially. I also demoted her by hiring a new manager, which infuriated her. I tolerated all her disrespect and bad behavior because I was taught to honor thy mother and thy father regardless of what they say or what actions they've taken against you.

I settled into my new location and immediately went to work at rebuilding my retail business. I ordered signs with the store policies and displayed them visibly. I held meetings with all employees to go over the daily operations and expectations. Ms. Brown did not attend the meetings and tried to continue her bad practices that previously got us into financial trouble. She argued with me in front of everyone, especially when I enforced the policies with her favorite customers. She argued with the other employees and wanted them to go against the policies when I wasn't around.

Ms. Brown resented me taking back control. She wanted me to pay off the financial disaster she'd created and then go away. Then she would go back to how she'd previously managed everything. She fought with me every step of the rebuilding process.

Ms. Brown's tactics included bullying and disrespecting me until I abdicated my responsibilities and sequestered in New Jersey as I did in 2003. Being in her presence daily proved difficult for me emotionally and physically. I developed a backache that wouldn't go away, despite my monthly chiropractic adjustments. Being around her made me feel like that scared little girl who landed in America. I was losing this battle because I engaged in her unloading tactics instead of my soul's strategy. I was reactionary. I charged forward when she charged forward. This pattern of unhealthy unloading wouldn't be easy to eradicate because it had been engrained in our DNA for generations. Retreating wasn't an option for me. Retreating meant voluntarily opening the door to depression's room and taking a seat.

I had to step back from my store a couple of days out of the week to tend to my wounds from our battle. On my days away from my store, the thoughts about this pattern consumed me. I pitied myself because I felt I didn't deserve any of it since the day I was born. I deserved a better mother. Then speaking to another friend one afternoon intensified my desires. My friend had thrown her husband out of their home after finding out he was communicating inappropriately with another woman. She became a wreck, and depression controlled her days. She loved her husband but couldn't get over what he had done. One day, while waiting after school for our children, I asked her how she was doing.

My friend said, "I wasn't having a good day today, so I called up my mother and said, 'Mom, this is not a good day.'" Her mom listened to her and said words of love and encouragement. Her mother sat on the phone with her until she felt better. This made her day better too. What my friend detailed had opened my invisible book of woes and bookmarked the chapter titled "Mom."

As I continued listening, I secretly wished Ms. Brown and I had that kind of relationship, where I could call her up and simply say "Mom, this is not a good day," and she would listen to me and give me words of love and encouragement. And my day would be better too. I desperately wanted a mother like my friend's. *Why don't I have a mother like hers that I could lean on?* I screamed on the inside.

I'd been utterly embarrassed to tell anyone the truth of what went on with me and Ms. Brown. I stroked the imaginary pages with a blue highlighter as I continued listening to my friend laud over her mother. I hung onto her every word and continued highlighting what I lacked in my relationship with Ms. Brown.

I had felt rather good that day before the conversation with my friend, but awareness will disrupt your mood so that you will confront something you were afraid to look at. It was important to take a deep, honest look at my relationship with the woman that birthed me. I had to accept that Ms. Brown and I did not have a good relationship and may never be an ideal mother-daughter. The disruption was the impetus to facing the toxicity that had settled inside of me.

I wanted to run away from my store. Mainly I wanted to run

away from this war. But I desperately wanted to take my life back. So, I engaged Ms. Brown whenever we were together in the store. This was the only place where Marlon and my children were not present. I didn't want my children to know that their grandmother who loved them unconditionally didn't love her own daughter unconditionally and treated her terribly. I didn't want Marlon to know that his mother-in-law whom he loved and respected wasn't who he thought she was. I tried my best to protect everyone, including Ms. Brown.

In May 2007, I went against my gut feeling and opened my second retail establishment, Premium Fashions. Rebuilding Prominent Fashions had surpassed my expectations, and I wanted to increase my finances. I felt I could do this with my secret spiritual life to sustain me, but I was wrong. It wasn't long before overseeing both stores became physically and intellectually draining, and I even grew listless spiritually. Depression still hovered, but I was managing it, barely.

To keep myself hydrated with energy, I would escape to the suburban area of Mount Vernon to be alone at least for a few hours. I drove around until I found a quiet block where I could park under a large tree. Then I would crawl in the back seat of my Toyota Sienna and lay down. I listened to spiritual/self-help teachers on CDs, read their books, or talked to God. Sometimes I cried or roamed the area if it was sunny or sat in a park nearby.

I desperately wanted to feel purposeful. I had always had a strong inclination to help humanity, but I first needed to help myself. During one of my brief escapes in my car, while reading, I thought about spiritual teachers who were helping people find purpose. *How do they know what they know?*

The question seemed to trigger my unique tone because suddenly, I heard it swirling around me—that white noise that comes out of nowhere through my ears. I was becoming familiar with its communication but didn't know what specifically brought it on. Whilst sporadic in nature, I learned from past experiences to be still and let the sound envelop me. As we began getting to know each other, I would get overly excited by my tone's presence, only to have it go silent—an opportunity for relief I had lost and desperately wanted back. I felt uneasy for days whenever that happened.

I closed my eyes, taking slow, silent deep breaths. *What are you trying to say to me?* I asked calmly in my mind, knowing my unique tone would abandon me if I asked too forcefully. The intensity of the tone increased while I remained still and focused on the sound. *Please show me,* I begged.

My unique tone touched me in ways I'd never felt before. And my tears lubricated my lashes as the tone escaped through the outer corners of my eyes down the side of my face. I didn't want the sensation to end. The palms of my hands tingled, spreading to my arms and legs. The book slipped away from my right hand onto the floor mat. I became conscious of my breathing and the sharp rise and fall of my chest. I expanded upon each rise and felt weightless on each fall. The volume of my unique tone increased, and the world around me vanished. I no longer heard the birds cawing or cars going by. Instead, I felt God's harmonious, infinite arms wrap around me and gently pull me into His hallowed place again. God's sacredness wouldn't allow for my mere existence to coexist, so I let myself fade away as I nestled into Divinity's security blanket and let go.

I emerged blissfully from this ineffable space with an answer: *Those spiritual teachers were following their soul's intentions* was the message I heard. I understood in that moment that I needed to be in tune with my soul to know its intentions.

By now, I was beginning to feel unhappy attending church as my beliefs were no longer aligned. I constantly questioned and opposed its teachings. These teachings no longer resonated with me. I'm not sure if they ever did. I could not be in line with my soul and understand its intentions if I stayed. That was the answer

I found for myself. In the New Year of 2008, I began disconnecting from Charm's story and gave up religion altogether.

I knew this would be a difficult step on my way to Kadian given that Grandma and Ms. Brown had been members for almost twenty years and were devoted to their faith. I noticed this was another area of my life where Ms. Brown had control of me. I'd been wanting to renounce religion for a while but couldn't muster enough courage to do so because I was afraid of her reaction. Also, I had forced my family there and felt obligated to stay. After explaining my views on the matter, my children and Marlon were fine with my choice, but they opted to continue attending. I respected their decision to stay members as I learned this was my path and not theirs.

Only a couple of months later, my family also left the church. They had concluded that attending church wasn't their choosing and was not in alignment with their own beliefs and values. My family's decision saddened Grandma and infuriated Ms. Brown. They felt I should be the one to set an example and keep everyone there. They hadn't realized I *was* setting an example. I was teaching my family to follow their own inward guidance. My children later told me that they did not like being forced to attend, especially my son. Learning the lesson of not forcing someone on your path and not deciding for others was a huge step for me.

I began taking control back slowly. Ms. Brown seemed angry with me every second of the day. Imagine someone being angry at you because they are losing control over your life.

By the end of 2008, I felt exhausted by the constant fights with Ms. Brown. I thought leaving her to work at Prominent Fashions while I managed Premium Fashions would keep her occupied and ease the tensions between us, but it did not. She would call me on the phone to argue, and when I wouldn't engage, she stormed to Premium Fashions to have it out in person with me. She continued to disregard my policies, such as by making deals behind the back of my employees and me with the customers she deemed her special friends, meaning almost anyone who walked into my store. I would find out when these customers came back expecting special favors.

It was December 30, the last business day of 2008, and we were extremely busy. Both stores did great in sales, and I had no interactions with Ms. Brown. It seemed like I was going home peacefully. But then the manager of Prominent Fashions called about fifteen minutes before closing to complain about my mother.

One of Ms. Brown's friends had bought a dress three months prior and wanted to exchange it for a different dress because she had an event to attend. The manager observed the item had no tags on it and looked worn. Our policy is clearly stated by the cash register: NO REFUND, EXCHANGE ONLY WITHIN TWO WEEKS. TAGS MUST BE ON ITEMS AND NOT WORN. It was the same policy as every establishment on the block that sold similar merchandise. While the manager was describing the situation to me, I could hear Ms. Brown carrying on in the background. I told my employee I would come down and straighten out the situation.

Seeing me enter Prominent Fashions infuriated Ms. Brown and she fell into her pattern of disrespect and shouting. She knew what the outcome was going to be. I gave the customer the bad news after examining the merchandise. When it was evident that she was not going to be granted the exchange, she gave a flippant remark, took her worn merchandise, and left. Ms. Brown and I continued arguing.

"I'm trying to figure out what could you possibly gain by taking back worn merchandise that cannot be sold again!"

"It wasn't worn. You and your manager are liars!" Ms. Brown shouted loud enough so that the manager could hear from the loft. "Do you think a good Christian woman who is devoted to her faith would do such a thing?"

"Besides the fact that it's beyond the exchange date and has no tags on it, do you consider yourself a good Christian woman, carrying on the way you do?" I snapped back.

My question enraged Ms. Brown to such an apoplectic dispro-portion that I had to take a step back from her. We continued the back-and-forth exchange. Engaging with her tactics exhausted me. Patterns will wear you down. I was befallen in battle. Without the energy to continue, I stopped engaging her. I held back the tears, took a quick, deep, shuddered breath, and looked towards the loft.

I was about to throw in my flag when everything seemed almost frozen in time—the walls of the store pulsed in slow motion. Ms. Brown continued screaming, but the pulsation increased its volume, drowning out her voice.

I felt myself leaving yet present at the same time. I was there and not there. My voice was muzzled in this space, like being in a dream unable to scream as the store faded out of focus. I was the focal point in a picture as the scene of our argument became a blurred background. Awareness had inserted itself between us.

The scenery juxtaposed onto a vision of my future that terrified me. I saw older versions of Ms. Brown and myself yelling at each other. Nothing had changed. We were locked in a generational pattern and headed in the same direction as she and Grandma until the day we discarnate.

I didn't know how long I was caught up in the noticing, but when I came out of it, Ms. Brown was still quarreling. "You don't know how to run a goddamn store."

I couldn't bear what I had observed, so I pointed to Ms. Brown, shouting, "I won't give you what you want."

"What do you think I want?" she barked back.

"You want for our relationship to be like yours and Grandma's and I won't give you that!"

Ms. Brown stood there stunned by my reply and said nothing more. I told my manager to lock up and bring me the keys. Then I flounced off to Premium Fashions to close up for the year.

When my manager arrived with the keys, I apologized as usual for Ms. Brown's bad behavior. "Thank you for your patience. I will

figure something out soon," I said, reassuring her that things
would soon change.

"Gosh, I hope you do very soon. This is so toxic and bad for
business," she replied. I took the keys from my manager, wished
her a happy new year, got in my car, and drove off.

The vision disturbed me. I did not want to end up treating Ms.
Brown the way she treated her mother. I banged on the steering
wheel of my car and tearfully shouted, "Fuck! I don't want this for
us!" It didn't seem like there had been any improvement in our
relationship. We were ending the year the same way we had
started it.

I had to pull over to the side of the road as my emotions overtook me. I thought about the foresight that had seeped through
earlier of Ms. Brown and I arguing in our senior years. I couldn't
unsee it. The awareness had awakened me to a possible outcome
for us and my future generations. The thought of my children and
I interacting this way wrung my insides bone-dry and left me with
an unquenchable thirst for change.

I didn't want that future. The impending outcome scared me.
*How can this relationship with Ms. Brown be repaired? Is she going
to die or am going to die before we figure this shit out?* I took deep
breaths to calm myself. After a few minutes, I put my car in drive
and continued home.

I felt tingling in my toes as I approached the ramp towards the
George Washington Bridge. My soul was readying itself to commu-
nicate with me, and I reluctantly gave it my attention. I was still
tense about the earlier awareness, which contradicted my usual
reaction to our interactions. I felt the sensation rising up my legs as
I neared the bridge over the Hudson River. The tingling filled my
being, and I heard a mild, whispery voice.

"Be still and know that I am God."

The bridge opened up, and my car plunged in the Hudson
River below. A small part of the three-mile-wide river formed a
glove around my car and safely rested it at the bottom. Submerged,
I watched my anger, concerns, and fears about this situation being

carried away by the river until they were no longer visible. My car and I reemerged on the New Jersey side of the Hudson anew, baptized with a new belief: Ms. Brown and I would not succumb to this generational pattern.

I may have fallen in the river symbolically, but when I drove over the Hudson River into New Jersey via the George Washington Bridge, I literally felt this stuck pattern loosening and freeing itself. My taut shoulders were now relaxed, and energy returned to my tired body. The drive home wasn't so daunting anymore because I had hope. There was a change that would impact posterity. I didn't know the details of the change yet, but something felt different about the future with Ms. Brown and me and my children.

"Be still and know that I am God" is my favorite Bible verse. Communication from the soul will connect through familiarity; for instance, a phrase you love. I knew something greater than Ms. Brown and I had come in between us earlier that evening and was assisting me.

I was not the same person who had entered Prominent Fashions perturbed by Ms. Brown's attitude, due to the awareness that had burrowed its way into my consciousness. I caught sight of my own metamorphosis in progress stemming from my vision and felt the difference between the current me and a greater version of myself. What emerged from the bottom of the Hudson River was my greater potential, and I entered the New Year with renewed hope and inspiration to continue. From that moment on, I turned towards the beckoning call of my soul.

CHAPTER EIGHT

Generational Patterns and Family Secrets

I was standing behind the register helping a customer choose an evening bag when Grandma and Ms. Brown came into Premium Fashions, thumping in unison through the store.

"Fay, I asking you to take me to the supermarket and to the bank tomorrow," Grandma insisted disrespectfully of Ms. Brown.

My grandmother was feisty, demanding, and headstrong. At eighty years old, she lived alone and took care of herself by choice.

"Hi Charm," Grandma greeted me and aimed for her usual spot. It was her habit to sit in the middle seat in the row of chairs centered in the store. A lot of my customers knew my grandmother because she visited with me at the store regularly, and they all called her Grandma.

"Good day," Grandma said to the lady standing at the counter.

"Good day, Grandma. You look strong today."

"Thank you, I feel great. I brought us seasoned rice with ackee for lunch," said Grandma.

"Thank you, Grandma," I said with a smile. Jamaican seasoned rice made with ackee is one of my favorite dishes.

"Oh boy, I could sure eat some, Grandma. Did you bring enough for me?" the lady joked.

"I didn't know you'd be here. Next time," said Grandma.

"You made it here before it started pouring outside, Grandma," I said.

"Yes, and the rain is setting up to do some damage today!"

Ms. Brown did not greet me or the customer. She marched to my office to put our lunch on my office table. I could tell she and Grandma had been having it out before they arrived.

"Ma, I can't tomorrow. I'm working a double today and would like to go home and get some sleep when I get off work in the morning," said Ms. Brown as she stood by office door, continuing the argument that had preceded before entering the store.

Ms. Brown is a licensed practical nurse and worked for a nursing home. She was scheduled to work from 3 p.m. to 11 p.m. and 11 p.m. to 7 a.m.

"But I need to pay my bills and buy food," Grandma complained, setting to pitch a fit as usual.

My Grandma is a stickler for paying her bills on the first of the month. This day is an adventure in itself. The adventure kicks off with Grandma going into the bank to withdraw cash and chat with her favorite teller to catch up on things. She does not use an ATM or want a cell phone. She also won't let anyone go pay the bills without her to either. The computer age is difficult for her generation to adjust to. Afterwards, Ms. Brown takes her to Con Edison to pay her electricity bill, then to the realtor across from Con Edison to pay her rent. Off to the phone company to pay her landline. Grandma sometimes stops at the pharmacy to refill her medication. Then to the supermarket to buy groceries, which can take hours. Grandma strolls up and down the aisles, reading the labels of each product she might buy even though she always gets the same items.

If the first of the month falls on a day Ms. Brown is available, then there's no argument. Otherwise, the manipulation, lying, and shaming begins when Grandma can't get her way with Ms. Brown.

"Ma, we can go the day after when I'm off from work. You have enough food in your refrigerator until then."

"You are no help to me," Grandma barked at her. "I have to beg you every month to help me. Why I have to beg you for help?"

"You have three other children and lots of grandchildren that live close by. Call one of them to go with you. I can't go tomorrow!" Ms. Brown shouted in frustration.

The rain pelted down on the roof of the building and slapped the pavement outside as if it too was frustrated with Grandma's impatience and unreasonable request.

"Don't tell me who to ask! It's a goddamn shame when you have to beg your own child to help you."

I stopped helping the customer for a second and glared at Grandma. She knew what that look meant. She rolled her eyes at me and stopped talking. I resumed helping the customer.

The lady found an evening bag to her liking, paid for it, and rushed towards the front door. "I'll hold you to lunch next time Grandma. Let me run before the storm gets any worse. Good day, everyone."

We all said goodbye to the customer individually, watching her hurry out of the store.

"You're not worth having," Grandma continued, insisting on having the argument so she could get her way as usual.

"I'm the only one that helps you and because you can't wait one day, I'm not worth having? Since I'm not worth having, call your other children then," replied Ms. Brown. "I'm going home after work tomorrow to get some rest."

"Fuck off and don't tell me who to ask. If you don't fucking want to help me, then just say so. I'm not going to beg you anymore."

The wind screeched in the vestibule of Premium Fashions as if it was appalled by Grandma's statement. The three of us looked towards the front of the store somewhat startled but relieved that everything remained intact.

"You're just a selfish bitch!" hollered my harridan grandmother.

"Stop it now! Grandma, you're out of line," I scolded.

Grandma sucked her teeth and kept quiet.

Ms. Brown scurried past me at the register with a waddling gait caused by an old ankle injury. "You expect me to do everything for you, but I couldn't live in your house like everyone else. You only sent for me when you needed me to babysit your children and clean your house."

"What?" I whispered, flummoxed by Ms. Brown's reply. I turned away from the computer at the register and glanced her way.

Ms. Brown sucked her teeth and stormed out of the store into the rain.

Ms. Brown almost never talked about her childhood, so her statement stunned me. For the first time, I realized Ms. Brown had a story without me in it. My story had been from one perspective only: mine. I never considered Ms. Brown's life before I was born. Ms. Brown's statement ushered in a new awareness for me, and I began to wonder what happened in her childhood.

When Ms. Brown left, I sat next to Grandma to inquire.

Incredulous, I asked, "Grandma, my mother didn't live with you when she was a child?"

"No, she lived with Mama."

"Why?"

Grandma let out a sigh. "Well, you know, in those days, Charm, your parents took care of your children because you were too young or if the father wasn't around. Your mother didn't have a father."

Grandma continued to justify her position. "Fay spent time with us during the holidays. I made sure she went to a good school, and she didn't want for anything. I gave money to Mama and brought her things every weekend."

"Grandma, that's a poor excuse." My annoyance bubbled to the surface. "My mother must have felt unloved by you."

Grandma didn't say anything. She just sighed and looked down at the pink flamingo carpet.

Ms. Brown's anger towards her mother instantly became clear.

She was pain-ridden from Grandma's lack of care and acknowledgment towards her.

Premium Fashions fell quiet with Ms. Brown gone, when only moments earlier, Grandma's temper and the tempest had been battling it out. I looked towards the front of the store and noticed the storm had passed on and had taken Grandma's anger with it.

I continued to probe my grandmother. "When did my mother live with you?"

"When she was a teenager."

"Why was she allowed to live with you then?"

Grandma lifted her eyes from the carpet and looked towards my office. "Her sister was sickly, and I needed help with her and the house."

"Grandma, you treated my mother like a babysitter and a housekeeper instead of a daughter!"

Grandma returned her gaze to the carpet in shame. Her left-hand starting twitching. I put my right hand in her left hand and clenched them together. Then I put my head on Grandma's left shoulder. She patted my head with her right hand while valiantly fighting back tears. The silence amplified our breathing, and the store seemed to disintegrate for a moment. Silence proffers wisdom to those who would listen. Grandma began humming "Blessed Assurance." I knew she was thinking of her mother because that was Mama's favorite hymn.

"Grandma, do you want to talk to my mother about this situation, so she'll have a better understanding and maybe she won't be so angry with you?" I asked softly.

Grandma shook her head and said in a faint whisper, "No, Charm. We mustn't talk about the things that have happened to us. We're just supposed to forgive them."

Just then, a customer entered the store to buy a pair of nursing shoes. I didn't want to leave my grandmother's side, but I had to tend to the customer.

"Hello Grandma," the lady said cheerily.

Grandma didn't respond. She stayed with downcast eyes and

continued humming. I'm not certain that she heard the customer greet her. Looking a little disappointed, the lady focused on the nursing shoes I had on display and quickly found a style she liked. While cashing her out, the lady turned to my grandmother and said, "Grandma, you're not your usual perky self today."

Still no response from Grandma. The lady turned to me to ask if Grandma was doing all right. I said, "Yes, she and I were having a painful talk."

"Oh! Those are difficult but necessary at times. Enjoy your day." She turned to Grandma before leaving the store and said, "Your day will get better Grandma. Keep the faith."

I sat back down next to Grandma. I put my head on her shoulder. After a few minutes, Grandma spoke. "You know, Charm, my mother allowed them to take me away."

I raised my head and turned to look at Grandma. "Who took you away, Grandma, and why would Mama allow it?"

Grandma rolled her eyes and bit her lip, trying not to burst into tears. "There's so much you don't know. So much."

"I want to know, Grandma. Please tell me. I want to comprehend the dysfunctions in this family so we can stop repeating them."

Grandma gently patted her cane and began telling me about her beginnings. "My father's side of the family were half Scottish and half Black. That's why you have freckles, Charm. My father's mother had lots of freckles. His sisters had freckles. Even though some of us have a tiny bit of freckles around the center of our faces and noses, you're the only one in the family that has freckles like them. My father was educated and a man of upper class. He dated Mama, who was poor, uneducated, dark-skinned, and made a living selling goods at the market. His family felt she was beneath him."

Grandma took a breath, and I sat back in the chair.

"My father's family didn't like my mother, and shortly after I was born, they took me from her."

Still fighting back tears, Grandma spoke in a cracked voice,

"My mother let them take me. They didn't tell me anything good about my mother when I lived with them. They kept telling me with disdain how uneducated and poor she was."

I took hold of Grandma's left hand, and she continued, "I didn't look like them. They had red hair and piercing blue and gray eyes with freckles. I was born with their eye color. I felt uncomfortable around them."

"Where was Pops?" I asked. Pops was the name we called my great-grandfather, Grandma's father.

"He lived in town and traveled a lot for work. Pops traveled to Panama and Aruba. He worked on the Panama Canal. Once he was gone for a whole year while I lived with his people. I hated living with them."

"How long did you live with them, Grandma?"

"I think I was almost seven years old when Mama finally came for me. She didn't want them raising me anymore."

"It sounded like you were angry with Mama."

Grandma did not respond to my statement.

"Did you forgive Mama?"

After a few moments, Grandma said, "Aahie sah." It's a Jamaican term that can have many meanings depending on the context. In this case, it was a sigh of relief and at the same time meant "Oh God."

Then she said, "I tried to."

Grandma resumed humming "Blessed Assurance" while slightly rocking her head from side to side. A tear broke free and sought refuge on the second knuckle of my index finger. Seconds later, another escaped and splatted next to the knuckle of my middle finger and slowly ran down my hand. Then another. And another. Then, in a soft, warbling voice, she sang, "This is my story, this is my song. Praising my Savior, all the day long. This is my story, this is my song. Praising my Savior, all the day long."

She unloaded differently. This was the first time I'd seen my grandmother express herself without being out of control. She didn't exert anger to cover up her pain. She went below her anger and expressed her real emotions gently. This was a healthier way of unloading and unusual for her.

I sat with Grandma quietly and gave her the space to surface her emotions. I didn't want to judge her for her mistakes. In that moment, I wanted her to have some relief. I hoped she could let go of some of her regrets.

"It's okay, Grandma," I said after a few minutes. "We've all made mistakes."

I held my grandmother's hand as she continued singing her mother's favorite hymn. Every tear, sniffle, and sigh began shifting the ground below this stubborn generational pattern that has been traveling through time, cohabitating with at least four generations. The omnipresent sound of her voice pulled me into her story and revealed an awareness that I observed with an amount of incredulity at first. Mama wasn't the perfect human being I had thought her to be. She had hurt her daughter.

I remembered their arguments as a child. Mama often walked on eggshells around Grandma. I wondered if she regretted giving her daughter up for the short time. Did she understand Grandma's anger towards her? Did she ask for her daughter's forgiveness when she prayed? I sighed and wondered what else I didn't know about this difficult relationship.

When I was born, Mama was almost seventy years old, so I don't have a full perspective on this relationship. I can only speak to what I observed the first six years of my life and when I visited during the summers until Mama died.

Grandma often said insulting things to her mother. She cursed, screamed, and called Mama names during their disagreements. I was often angry with Grandma for treating Mama this way, unaware of the pain she had tucked away deep inside for almost ninety years.

Mama died at seventy-nine years old and didn't ease her daughter's pain or eradicate the pattern. Grandma died at ninety-one years old and didn't attempt to eradicate the pattern with

Ms. Brown. Neither of them ever found a healthier way to unload past and ongoing emotional trauma.

I knew Pops. He stood tall with a slender build. I could recall his light-skinned, handsome face and his curly hair. He had a gentle, poised, and charismatic demeanor. He used to come by Grandma's house every Sunday and sometimes during the weekday. Pops played with my brothers and me when he visited. He would pick us up and spin us around. He had a spectacular smile. He always brought us things, like delicious fruits or toys. Once he brought me a slate with white chalk. Pops showed me how to write my name on my slate and how to count with the abacus beads. His eyes were full of love and glistened when he looked at us.

Pops always sat and talked with Mama. They laughed a lot together. I enjoyed watching Mama throw her head back and burst out with laughter when they were in conversation. They had a connection. I can even say they had love for each other. Then there were times when Mama seemed upset with him and didn't want to see him at all. But he always came to see us regardless. Even now, I wonder if Mama was still hurt that he didn't choose her.

My parents, brothers, and I visited Pops when we returned to Jamaica when I was nine years old. He didn't recognize us at first. He had dementia by then and slipped in and out of different realities. We sat with him on his verandah, and Ms. Brown held his hands and spoke lovingly to him. His eyes were lackluster in a way that was unfamiliar to me. Then for a moment, the Vastness returned him to us, and he remembered who we were. His eyes lost their dullness to reveal that glisten we were used to. "Fay, you're here," he said.

Ms. Brown hugged and kissed him. He kissed my brothers and I and remembered our names too. Then he would disappear back into the Vastness. When he was present again, he would talk to us. Pops pointed to the woman in the yard and said, "That's my sister." With her red hair and freckles, she didn't look biracial like Pops.

I don't know if they had different fathers and I didn't inquire. She didn't speak or gesture towards us; she just stared.

Pops had grandnieces and nephews who were visiting from England when we arrived. Some might have been great grand-nieces, given their ages. The children came over to us and spoke. "Top o' the morning to you." How strange that sounded yet how beautiful their accents were. Some of them had freckles like me. But they were quickly ushered away by other adults and not allowed to speak to us anymore. We were referred to as "Pops' side of the family."

Ms. Brown did not know her father. He was never part of any conversations growing up. I don't know if she wondered about him. I never thought about him, and I am sure my brothers didn't either. But we were destined to meet.

Ms. Brown bought her first house in August 1985, a block away from the Dyre Avenue train station in the Bronx. Grandma was in Jamaica for a lengthy stay when we moved in. She had missed her husband, family members, and the island that she loved so much. She returned to America around November.

In January 1986, my brothers were hanging out with some of their friends by the Dyre Avenue station. They were engaged in a dispute when an older gentleman intervened and squashed the argument before it could escalate. Whenever the older gentleman visited the Caribbean franchise on the corner of Dyre, he would stop to talk with my brothers for a moment if he saw them.

One day, Grandma was on her way to Ms. Brown's house and saw the old man talking to my brothers. They were both stunned when their eyes met.

"What are you doing here, Mackie?" Grandma asked the gentleman from her past.

"I was on my way to buy groceries at the Caribbean store when I saw these boys misbehaving. I stopped to counsel them," he responded. "Do you live around here?"

"No, but your daughter does. She lives around the corner."

The man became motionless because he understood who Grandma was talking about. My brothers, still unaware of what was happening, were uninterested in the conversation.

"Do you know who these young men are that you are counseling?" asked Grandma.

"No. I'm just trying to keep them out of trouble."

"Well, they're your grandchildren. They are your daughter's sons," Grandma said.

My brothers stood there with eyes bugged out and mouths agape. "What?" one said.

"Grandchildren?" asked the other.

After a few moments, my grandfather asked if he could have Ms. Brown's address and phone number. Grandma gave it to him. But he didn't call right away.

Sometimes a situation comes in our life that may seem like luck or happenstance, but I don't believe in either. I think we draw unto ourselves what we desire most. Synchronicity's unexpected nature is to breathe hope into our lives. It greets us when we are not looking. Being on my spiritual path and learning about desires, I wondered if this meeting was a deep desire of my mother or grandfather or both.

Grandfather finally got the courage to call. I invited him to dinner the following Sunday because it was Ms. Brown's day off, and he accepted. We all welcomed him, except Grandma, who was annoyed by his presence. Ms. Brown seemed happy to know her father. I invited him back the following Sunday.

One Sunday, with only Grandma, Grandfather, and myself in the house, I asked him the question to chase the elephant out of the room. "Why weren't you a part of my mother's life?"

"Charm, I'm going to tell you the truth, but your grandmother won't like it."

My grandmother began to sigh, and I scolded her before she could stop him from explaining. Grandfather said that he had only slept with my grandmother once when she got pregnant. He liked the way she titivated herself, but her cantankerous and vulgar nature turned him off. He couldn't have a relationship with someone like that. Grandma chased him away because he didn't want a relationship with her, only with his daughter.

"Every time I stopped by the bar to see my daughter, she yelled profanity at me. The last time she hurled a rum bottle at me and said not to come back."

He turned to his one-year-old daughter and said, "You'll never see me again." And he left.

My grandfather continued. He said that one day in early February of 1967, his friend saw him and asked, "Hey, you know that lady that has your daughter? The lady that owns the bar and grill?"

"Yeah," answered Grandfather.

"Her daughter just had a baby. Your daughter had a baby."

Willing to put everything aside to make contact with his daughter and granddaughter, he arrived at Grandma's house with gifts for Ms. Brown and me. He said Grandma spat at him, threw the gifts in his face, and told him to never come back. Ms. Brown didn't know that he came to see us until he revealed to me what happened that Sunday. When I asked my Grandma why she kept my mother's father from her, she had no answer for me. She just glared at Grandfather.

I don't know what he was like as a young man, but the man I met was a soft-spoken, gentle person who abhorred profanity. He was very loving, supportive, and encouraging. I was blessed to know him, and I know my mother was happy about the time she spent with her father. Grandfather stayed in our lives until he died in 2004.

I wondered if he had been a part of my mother's life whether that would've changed who she became. If he had been a part of our lives from when I was days old, could he have set a different example of parenting for my mother?

. . .

In my late twenties, a few family members, myself, and Ms. Brown sat around after a family gathering talking about past childhood incidents. Most seemed innocent enough and made us laugh—until Ms. Brown told of an eerie incident that happened to her when she was almost a teenager. Grandma had called her to the kitchen to help her with dinner. She must have done something wrong because Grandma chopped her on her widow's peak with a cook spoon, and blood came gushing out of her forehead.

Stupefied by her story, I had to take a few deep breaths, almost gasping for air. I sat there in disbelief as juxtaposed memories of our gaping widow's peaks came into view. I envisioned my mother's hand inching to her forehead to touch it the way I had when she struck me as a child. I wondered if she felt woozy from the blow. Did her heart flutter from the shock? Her telling of this story sent me traveling back in time to relive this pattern with her. I kept forcing myself to breathe as I wondered about Ms. Brown's lack of empathy.

Then she continued, "I have the scar underneath my hair."

Ms. Brown told this story nonchalantly and even laughed about it. I don't know if she even remembered what she had done to me. Did she repress the memory of it? I never discussed this incident with Ms. Brown or questioned her that day. I didn't want to get into it. I wanted it to stay buried.

Ms. Brown often displayed anger towards her mother, especially in the last two decades of her mother's life. She did the things she felt obligated to do as a daughter. She made certain that her mother kept up with her health, ran errands for and with her, threw her birthday parties, and helped Grandma tremendously in her life. But all the years of abuse and control came out in the form of rage whenever they were together. Their disagreements were horrible—full of yelling and name-calling without resolutions. As one regurgitated their feelings, the other one swallowed them, and the cycle continued.

Ms. Brown treated me the way her mother treated her. Just as Grandma was unkind to my mother, my mother was unkind to me.

Patterns weren't eradicated, and they spilled onto our relationship.
Ms. Brown never tried to change the patterns between herself and
her own mother or between herself and me. For many years, I
ignored my own feelings, ignored her bad behavior, and pretended
we had a good relationship. My hair covers the small indentation
in my forehead, but the wound never healed.

I don't remember crying much that Sunday. But revisiting this
memory, I had to come to terms with how I felt for Ms. Brown
honestly. I didn't like or love this woman. I don't know if I ever
did. I was only obligated to her. Love isn't compulsory.

Writing this book has finally helped me to admit the ultimate truth
I wasn't able to face my whole life: Ms. Brown was abusive to me. I
can now utter the words, "I have an abusive mother." If I had faced
the truth earlier, I would've hated her, so instead I'd say things like
"She was mean" or "She was a terrible mother."

I did not intend to write about some of my abuse or my family's
patterning in detail. I was feeling conflicted. I didn't want my
mother to be judged by others. There's no excuse for a person's bad
behavior, but Ms. Brown unloaded years of abuse onto me
emotionally, verbally, and physically because she was abused.
Because she didn't know how to go beyond her hurt, she continued
in the same entanglements with her own mother. She wasn't able
to separate from the situation to see what should've been glaringly
clear to her.

Writing about my abuse lay heavily on my mind for a while.
When I was writing about it in 2020, I had a visitation from
Grandma. I was awoken around 4:30 one morning and couldn't go
back to sleep. I was thinking about how Ms. Brown would feel
seeing my abuse detailed so vividly. With my left arm snuggled
under my head and my hand extended out, thinking about how to
soften this chapter, I felt someone put their hand in my hand and
clasp them together. This instantly brought tears. I was familiar

with interactions from the other side, so I wasn't frightened. I've been doing this since I was a child.

Streams of tears flowed down my arm and onto my pillow. It brought me back to when she told me about her childhood. "Hi Grandma," I whispered. She made her presence stronger. She conveyed that my book is meant to heal myself and that I should write my truth to heal myself and the family, the ones still here on Earth and on the other side.

She said, "Dying doesn't relieve you of karma you created on Earth. It's part of your soul print and will be part of another incarnation if not healed."

As I cried from her overwhelming support, her last words to me were, "I wasn't at my best. I want you to be brave and write your truth. This is not your shame to carry."

Then her presence evaporated.

CHAPTER NINE

An Inspiring Year

The last time I felt freedom was the night when my father threw me out in 1984. I ran like hell from his clutches, only to be caught in the snare of Ms. Brown's microcosm of life's modification and generational traumas. I was entrapped in her reality while attempting to create my own. The dissonance of both worlds disrupted my flow, and I often veered off course. I wished Ms. Brown could expel me from her reality the way my father expelled me from his. But she couldn't let me go even if she wanted to. Neither of us had the strength to begin breaking the cemented wall that had separated us since I was eleven years old. I wouldn't be free until I'd broken some of the generational patterns —until I picked up a sledgehammer and begin breaking down the wall. We needed each other for now. It seemed God himself was conspiring behind the scenes to help us unlock the chains that bound us together so our souls could take flight.

I sat on the floor of my family room wondering what the New Year would bring as 2009 said hello to me. I could hear Marlon on the phone with his brother wishing each other a Happy New Year. Kamilah was an adult now and out with friends. Khaleel and Kyra were watching television in their rooms, and I sat twisting my wedding ring, feeling trapped by what I had promised. I could sense my next potential self, but I couldn't quite step into her yet. It had been almost thirteen years since I was courageous enough to ask for a divorce. That was the last time I really felt like Kadian.

Unable to fall asleep, I turned on the television and cruised through the channels. I came upon *The Truman Show*, which had just started. Even though I'd seen the movie before, I watched it anyway. It is such a metaphor for life. I've felt like Truman many times. *The Truman Show* is a film about a man who, since birth, has lived in his own snow globe constructed by television writers, with everyone in the show aware of his fake life except him. He is watched by billions from around the world. Truman's life appeared perfect. The producers gave him the perfect wife, the perfect neighborhood to live in, good jobs for himself and his wife, a best friend, and material things, but he wanted more. The more he settled into his life, the more he felt the unsettling call of the Universe. This triggered Truman to embark upon a quest to find authentic happiness and truth.

Truman was feeling a strong yearning for more than what he was living in. He wanted an intimate, romantic relationship, a purposeful job, deeper relationships, adventure, and expansion of himself. He took the chance in a boat to cross deep waters (so he thought) to leave his life behind—even though he had a phobia for water—to find his authentic self and to be happy. He was willing to die for his deep desires. The one who deeply feels the call will risk even their own life for something new and exciting.

I retired for the evening when the movie ended. I sat on the edge of my bed for a moment twiddling my wedding band and wondered, *what am I willing to risk for my own personal happiness?* That night, I put my wedding ring in my second dresser drawer, and I never put it on again.

I laid in bed remembering how I felt when I chose things that made me feel good, like going to a soul retreat or reading spiritual books at a hotel by myself. If I was keeping my spiritual life a secret, then I was afraid to follow my heart. I was the one keeping the next potential version of myself away.

The first thing I did for myself in the New Year was to tell the landlord of my first store, Prominent Fashions, that I would not be renewing my lease for 2010. Then I hired a young lady to work part-time in my other store. The extra days away from my store allowed me to spend more time with my children and to delve into my personal interests.

Ever since I started seeing Dr. Schick, I'd been curious about alternative ways to heal the body. I never stopped my chiropractic care, but that year I investigated acupuncture, reflexology, massage, and other healing modalities. It reignited that verve I had found for unconventional therapies and teachings when I ended my weekend escapes. A whole world was out there with experiences I wanted to have. I began interacting with others around me who had similar interests. Conversations and sessions with them further expanded my spiritual capacity and my knowledge.

One friend began an interest in Shamanism, and I accompanied her to an appointment with a Shamanic healer to gain a better understanding of this practice. While my friend was in the middle of her session, the Shaman glanced my way from time to time. When my friend's session was over, he offered me a quick reading and healing of my energy. I was surprised by what he said during my mini session. One, I needed to deal with the dysfunctional relationship with Ms. Brown. Two, I should look into Reiki healing, And three, I am an author. I was astonished by his accurate reading of my relationship with Ms. Brown since he hadn't met me before. It was the first time I had heard of Reiki, and to be honest, I wasn't interested so I didn't follow up. And I thought he was incorrect about being an author because I'd had no interest in writing before. But one out of three wasn't bad, I thought.

I loved the buffet of bodily experiences the Universe provided, but my main focus was on matters of the soul. I wanted to be versed on this subject. While searching the internet for more information one evening, I clicked on a link for "Soul World." It was the website of author Ainslie MacLeod, who wrote *The Instruction: Living the Life Your Soul Intended.* His website posed intriguing questions, such as "Do you know your soul type? and "What is your soul age?"

This piqued my interest and compelled me to get his book for additional information. After reading it and doing all the exercises, I decided to have a session with Ainslie. Many interesting things happened during our first session, but two comments stuck out more than others. The first was he insisted that I sign up for a Reiki class, and the other: I was an author.

When I receive a message more than once from different individuals unrelated to each other, that means I need to listen. I was still unconvinced about writing, but I enrolled in a Reiki I class in Manhattan. Energy healing came as natural to me as breathing. I felt at home in my energy, perhaps for the first time since leaving Jamaica at six years old. Besides interacting with my own energy and the energy of others, Reiki offered another way to engage with my soul and intuition. It helped me to venture further out of my spiritual closet. I took Reiki II in the spring to advance my understanding of this modality that felt intrinsically normal and centered me. I practiced Reiki on my friends, my children, other family members, and mostly myself. My children especially loved it. It calmed them and me. I worked on myself before I went to bed and when I rose in the morning.

I wanted a deeper understanding of the connection between Reiki and intuition because I noticed how much more precise my intuition was becoming. I started listening to Marie Manuchehri on the radio, an intuitive energy healer in Washington whom I found through Ainslie's website. I was quite impressed with her skills and felt a strong push to have a session with her. I made an in-person appointment on faith and booked a flight to Seattle for a few months out. I didn't know where I'd stay or all the details surrounding this trip because I'd never been to Washington, but it didn't matter. I would figure that part out later.

People pushed back at my not-so-secret spiritual life now, especially Ms. Brown. This was extremely foreign to her and seemed almost blasphemous. I was constantly reminded about my absence from church and leading her grandchildren down the wrong path. Marlon was not fond of my new hobby either. He hoped it wouldn't become a lifestyle for me. He didn't interfere, nor did he want to talk about my new interests. I approved of his disinterest given he was no longer invited on my journey to my soul.

It was still difficult being around Ms. Brown even though we were seeing less of each other. I gained some ground on the battle-field, but there were times my inner fortress weakened in her pres-ence, and she was able to breach it. Whenever that happened, we would fall back into the old pattern of yelling at each other. Our interactions brought on negative emotions that didn't feel great, but I was no longer afraid to acknowledge them. If I ignored them, they'd just continue to fester. I worked on feeling and releasing my emotions. I cried, wrote my feelings down, walked, and took up the habit of screaming out loud in my car or at home when I was alone. Screaming was a spontaneous reaction that I developed after one of my confrontations with Ms. Brown. I would either cry or laugh afterwards, and it brought tremendous relief. But I wished for more than that now. I desired to step away from my life briefly. Something I hadn't done since 2004.

When an email came across with a mention about a Soul Safari in South Africa with Ainslie, I didn't hesitate and signed up. In October 2009, I took the boldest step of my life and went to South Africa with over twenty like-minded strangers. I'd started out in my late twenties on this perilous journey to my soul, with brief respites to a hotel a couple of miles from home to work on topics that interested me. Then I traveled three thousand miles to San Francisco to do the same thing in my late thirties. Now, in my forties, I became relentless and traveled eight thousand miles for ten days to do it again. It was the furthest I'd ever been in my life on my soul journey. But I had to choose me.

The children, Marlon, and I arrived at John F. Kennedy Airport early for my trip. I wanted to spend some time with my kids at the airport before boarding. Their happiness for me came with a hint of sadness. This would be the first time I'd be away from them for this length of time. I would miss them terribly but felt excited to go.

During my flight on South African Airways, I thought about Ms. Brown. I was tired of our fights. The way we engaged felt abnormal to me now. I did not want to end up treating Ms. Brown the way she treated her mother. I wanted something different for our relationship, and I didn't want either of us to die still caught up in this pattern. I thought about Truman and what I was willing to risk, a question I had pondered often that year.

Many times as a child I had wished Ms. Brown would have sympathy for me, and even sought it from her. As I got older, I wished she would have compassion. Ms. Brown seemed to have neither, at least not for me. She had sympathy for her nieces and nephews and showed compassion to them all the time. It was obvious she possessed the capacity for those emotions, but I couldn't understand why they weren't there for me. I never felt acknowledged or appreciated. I only got more and more abuse. I thought if she pitied me, she would stop her destructive behavior toward me. I didn't understand then that what I really wanted was for Ms. Brown to have empathy, not sympathy. But even sympathy would have sufficed.

As I got older and learned more about empathy, I often wondered if Ms. Brown's empathetic button was turned off or dialed down low when she was born. I also felt the same about my grandmother; they both lacked this emotion. Empathy allows you to put yourself in another's place whereas sympathy only sees pity. Ms. Brown was never able to sense what I was feeling while she was abusive to me. If she had, she would've remembered how she felt when her mother mistreated her.

I wondered for a long time what could flip the empathy switch within a person, and then I saw Ms. Brown's empathy switch light up, along with her compassionate nature, when Kamilah was born. Her capacity for love, empathy, and compassion increased with each of my children. Ms. Brown was a horrible mother to me but excelled in grandmothership to my children. She gave my children tons of love. It was the only reason I kept up appearances of our relationship. The question still in my head was, *Why couldn't I receive that from her?*

It felt like I should've been the obvious choice to expand Ms. Brown's heart the way a child does for a lot of first-time mothers, but I wasn't. And I didn't. I've concluded that sometimes a person's increase in capacity for love, empathy, and compassion may not be elicited through who we might expect. The Universe places embodied horizons on our earthly passage to evoke growth within all of us. For me, that person was my great-grandmother, Mama.

We've seen this in our family or in someone else's family where the grandparents love their grandchildren instantly. Grandchildren assume their grandparents had always been loving and also that way with their parent. I now realize that loving is one of the joys of the future generation—they are here to help the previous generation increase their heart space tremendously. My grandmother was kinder to me than she was to Ms. Brown, and she was even kinder and showed more love to my children. I am happy to see the side I wanted in a mother and to see her growth when she interacts with my children. I am embracing the possibility that my idealistic model of a mother may never exist in our relationship, but I enjoy observing Ms. Brown's relationship with my children.

For example, when my children were younger and Ms. Brown came to visit, they would argue over who got to sleep next to her. Ms. Brown would put Kamilah on her left side, Khaleel on her right side, and Kyra slept on her chest. I smiled observing them asleep in the bedroom. Even now, I am smiling. I love that memory of her and her grandchildren.

That fifteen-hour flight was the longest I'd ever been on an airplane. It was now 7:18 a.m. with one and a half hours before touching down in South Africa. I was getting restless. My thoughts zigzagged from my life back home to wondering who I was going to room with when I arrived in South Africa, but full of excitement nonetheless. (We were not to be made aware of our roommates beforehand, as a request by Ainslie.) I decided to give myself a mini Reiki session to minimize my anxiety. I put my seat back and focused on my breath. I put my right hand on my second chakra, my left hand on my third chakra, and closed my eyes.

Reiki made it easier to remove myself from this world, and within minutes, the humming sound that came through my ears surrounded me. *Hello, my unique tone!* My shoulders and the muscles in my face relaxed. Anger and pity were absent in this space. I sensed something else profound was present instead. I opened my eyes before it enveloped me because I was afraid I might have one of my normal reactions to what was present, like crying uncontrollably or my body shuddering. I didn't want to frighten anyone on the plane. I sat in my seat smiling and feeling the calibration of this energy. *Love,* I whispered to myself. As I looked out the window, I had an overwhelming feeling to forgive Ms. Brown. I had hardly thought about forgiveness before, and I knew that it was Kadian who wanted to forgive her. Briefly, I was able to separate from Charm to experience Kadian again. The Kadian who jumped into her mother's birth canal.

The desire to forgive soon waned as Kadian and I departed to our own worlds again because I hadn't stepped into her yet. But the consciousness of forgiveness had stenciled itself onto my current consciousness and illuminated a new path before me. It was the same sense I felt the night before I left Jamaica: Mama's covering of love that imprinted on my current consciousness to remind me of what authentic love feels like when I needed reminding.

I landed in South Africa, then got on a charter flight to Madikwe Game Reserve, which borders Botswana. Another safarian and I, along with the photographers and the two female pilots, were on the flight together. It was my first time on a small plane. I felt woozy the whole time as the plane dipped, swerved, and shook in the air. I thought about Marlon and how much he would have hated this experience. We landed on a dirt strip where a Jeep waited to take us to our final destination, Madikwe Safari Lodge.

We were greeted by the staff with a cool cloth and champagne, then a song. I leaned into the embrace of the warm welcome from my fellow travelers who came from the East Coast to the West Coast of the United States and Canada. We didn't tarry as our first encounter with the animals awaited us. Madikwe Game Reserve has been in operation since 1991 and is one of the largest game reserves, hosting over eight thousand animals of twenty-eight different species. I hopped in the Jeep and looked over at the staff waving us off.

The next day, we sat in an airy room at the lodge with Ainslie for our first Soul World workshop with a spectacular horizon as our backdrop. He started with a meditation, and I could feel myself going into that sacred space almost immediately. I took slow deep breaths as Ainslie's soft voice traveled away from me, and silence became our spiritual teacher. There was something in the beyond that I tried to reach for but felt restraint. It hadn't seemed within my spiritual grasp. When the meditation was over, Ainslie called in his spiritual partners (which he calls his guides, some might say angels or intuition) and our spiritual partners to enter the group space. A sudden gush of wind swept over the room, and I began to see colors around some people, mostly around their heads. I looked to the horizon and saw scintillating sparks of light with particles floating in the atmosphere. The whole room and its contents became unsolid and malleable. It was like viewing the world under a microscope and seeing its real substance. I learned in Reiki that was energy. Most of us felt the presence of the spiritual partners arriving. It was such a surreal moment. After our group discussion, we went on another game drive.

We were escorted to the Boma that evening for dinner. It was outdoors around a fire with candlelight. Before dinner, the staff serenaded us with beautiful African songs and dances. Africa. The Mother Land. What a fitting name for this place. Every moment there brings you closer to your internal home. It felt like I was a baby ship that found the mother ship, and I was part of the higher consciousness again. After dinner, we did another meditation. I saw a vision of myself walking on a winding road. I couldn't see a destination, and the road was long. I wondered if that represented my current track, wandering without guidance. It was an emotional evening.

The next day, we had our group discussion under an acacia tree with a perfect blue sky above us and the sound of God's nature all around us. The experience was just what I wanted to have as a child or when I was laying in my dorm room crying. I had never imagined having such an experience this year. If I hadn't chosen my heart's desires, I would have been sitting in my store desperately wanting change in my life. I know choosing yourself is a risk. You don't know where your decision will take you. But I'm so glad I didn't listen to the voices that still wanted to control me. The voices that wanted me to strive for their perception of happiness.

This workshop was about forgiveness. *Hmmm*, I thought, as I leaned into the teaching. It was no coincidence. I latched onto every word so I could fully step into Kadian, my potential. In the meditation during our evening workshop, I saw myself standing at the top of a long flight of stairs. I ventured down the steps, and the further I descended, the more I felt afraid. I stopped on the last step and froze. I couldn't fully commit. I was overtaken by fear and opened my eyes before Ainslie finished the meditation. I thought about the stairs and wondered what I was afraid of.

We spent hours the next day discussing forgiveness. A lot of people wanted to know how to get there. Ainslie gave us a few tools. We were told if we ever hurt someone to immediately apologize and move on from it. That was going to be a challenge for me. I know I couldn't do that with the amount of anger I possessed inside. During the next meditation, we had to list five people whom we wanted to forgive and repeat a saying Ainslie recited to us while thinking of each person on the list. The first name I wrote in my journal was Ms. Brown, then four more.

Nothing is a coincidence in life. I was in this exact space and moment for a reason. The awareness to forgive seeped into my consciousness first on the airplane. I sought to cultivate this new perspective to fulfill my desire of wanting a different relationship with my mother. I desperately desired to evolve from that angry version of myself. During the meditation, I was stuck on just one image, Ms. Brown. I did the whole meditation with her in my mind, and I wept profusely. My desire to be unconditionally forgiving towards her grew.

The forgiveness meditation happened on our last full day in Madikwe. I felt some stuck energy craving to move out of my body afterwards, and my roommate and I opted for a massage session instead of another game drive. We chatted while waiting for our massages. It turned out she lived in Seattle, Washington, and knew Marie, the energy intuitive I had booked the appointment with in January of the upcoming year. This young lady invited me to stay with her while I was in Seattle, offering to take me back and forth to my appointment and entertain me. Coincidence? I think not.

The masseuse came to our lodge, and I had the most spectacular massage on the terrace in the sun. When she was done, I felt lighter, as if the stuck energies had evaporated into the atmosphere. I then had one of the best naps—one of my top five naps of all time.

In the evening session of our last night in Madikwe, we did a meditation called "The Last Caress." We were to imagine people we wanted to forgive or thank, then touch their face gently with a caress, and say, "I love you," "Thank you," or "I forgive you." Ainslie explained that this meditation was created from the story "The Last Caress" in the book *House to House* by David Bellavia and John R. Bruning. The only person I wanted to do that with was Ms. Brown. I wanted to give that last caress to her. I wanted to forgive her, but the love part or the thank you part wasn't there yet. Sometime in the meditation, my brother Adrian popped into my head. Adrian and I hadn't been in contact much since Brian's death. His problem with abusing drugs had spiraled out of control, and we grew further apart. I said *I love you* over and over to his image.

Ainslie's numerous messages from his spirit guides resonated. "Depression can act as a block from being connected." Boy, do I know that one very well. "It's time for older souls to step up and start to make a difference, even in small ways." I've always sought to make a difference in this life somehow. "We all have a deep connection to Africa because it's like coming home. It's our place of origin. This is where our souls began." I felt that message the strongest the evening we were in the Boma. *I was home.* "If you start to overcome your fears and start connecting to your soul to be yourself, you will make a big difference in this world." This is my story. This is my song.

After three and half days in Madikwe, we went to our next destination, Cape Town. Besides the five-star camping, game drives twice a day, and great company, I learned more information about the soul and my existence in this lifetime. I loved being around others I could openly have discussions with about the soul, reincarnation, and other topics that interested me. I cried on the charter flight back to the airport in Johannesburg. I missed this place already. The peaceful, slow-paced life of South Africa is to die for. The lodge was exquisite along with the food and service. The hospitality of the staff was impeccable, and the ambiance of the country was beyond all expectations. I put on my headphones and turned on Garnett Silk's song "Hello Mamma Africa." I've heard this song many times before, but it now touched me in a different way. I loved Africa from the bottom of my heart.

We can be in tune with God's infinite, harmonious system in so many ways. Nature is the perfect example. The precious animals exemplified what we're missing in our daily lives. Physical interaction with them isn't necessary, only observation. I desired a world like theirs.

Animals are similar to us in many ways. For one, they are hard-working. I saw this in the male dung beetle that rolls manure into a ball, about one thousand times its body weight, to be used by the female to lay eggs. Guided by the Milky Way, the male rolls the ball it created to a specific destination while carrying the female on top. They were one of my favorite creatures to observe. They were so tiny but seemed so mighty as if they understand their purpose in life.

Animals are curious. I loved seeing the baby jackals lift their heads out of their hole to peer at the interesting people in awe of their cuteness, with mama nearby making sure we stayed our distance. When the zebra warned us not to intrude on his space by stomping his feet, we stayed away. Animals like privacy too. I saw many animals with agendas like ours and prospering effortlessly in their world.

Animals are a great representation of what is absent in our lives: the expression of our true essence. The menagerie of birds and fireflies with their own distinctive hues spelled freedom every time I looked at them. I was a bird that didn't know she had wings until recently. I have to learn how to use them. Meanwhile, I'm fledging around until I can put them in flight.

Animals are dissimilar to us in many ways too. They know how to stay in their own world. Like the lion that had just eaten, walking past me in an open Jeep, acting unaware of my presence because its appetite was fulfilled. It wasn't concerned about another goal but seemed focused on the present only, not on its next meal. The playful wild dogs spoke to me loudest about this. They ran around our Jeeps as if we did not exist. They did not growl or bark at us intruding upon their world. They simply went around us the way a stream flows around a rock in its way.

Or the baby elephants enjoying a bath unaware of our presence because their mother didn't allow us to change her babies' routine.

She stood between us and her babies, warning us to stay afar. What if we had that protection from our loved ones from the moment we arrived here? Allowing us to enjoy life without interruption from outside influences and protecting us while we discover ourselves on our own journey? Like Mama did.

I left South Africa with new friendships and a different mindset. I no longer wanted anger in my life. I no longer wanted to be angry with Ms. Brown. My anger stood in the way of forgiveness and love. In order to love Ms. Brown, I felt I had to forgive her. On the plane ride back, I could feel many intentions from my soul and set three goals for myself. 1) I will dissolve my second store in 2010 if my landlord agrees. 2) I will stand up to Ms. Brown in my way. 3) I will divorce Marlon within the next two years.

A week after I came back from South Africa, I asked the landlord of my second store for an early termination of my lease. He was very understanding. He said, "I am not surprised based on our conversations. That is a wise choice, and you are wise. Follow your dreams. This is not your destiny."

With my landlord's blessing, I began preparing to close both stores. There was much to do, so I got to work immediately. I went to my stores every day to assist in their closing. Ms. Brown disagreed with me about closing the stores and rudely overstated her opinions on matters, but I wasn't going to fall for her trappings. I needed to remain focused.

On December 31, 2009, with only thirty days left to close my first store, Ms. Brown and I went at it again. She had received her sixth parking ticket that week, and it was only Thursday. She would not feed the meter on time and refused to park in the twenty-four-hour parking lot only a block away, which cost only a couple of dollars per day. The expired meter tickets were costing me thirty to sixty dollars every other week. To avoid a confrontation, I'd give her the money when she fussed, but I was learning to stand in my power by standing up to her. Ms. Brown had many expectations of me as her daughter. I am expected to do as she says regardless of my age.

After she fell into her entitled rage in the store per usual, I left there discombobulated. I couldn't contain my anger, and so I pulled into the McDonald's when I crossed over the George Washington Bridge to cool off. In the drive-through, I ordered a soda, extra large.

I slipped one of my meditation CDs in my car radio, rested my seat back, and closed my eyes, hoping to diminish my anger. I couldn't focus, so after a few minutes, I ejected the CD and turned off my radio. To be honest, I didn't want the anger to dissipate. I wanted the anger to engulf me. So, I let it. My anger justified my actions in the argument. I seesawed between anger and self-pity. My seething anger was as soothing as the sugar in the soda.

After a short while, I got on the New Jersey Turnpike to head home. My phone rang when I was almost at my exit. I looked at the screen and saw that it was her.

"Hello," I said, annoyed.

"I'm calling to let you know a customer was complaining about the closing policy," Ms. Brown barked. "I think you should change it to be more accommodating. Like allowing them to exchange what they've purchased."

"I'm already offering a huge discount because I am closing. That's why they are allowed to try on anything before purchase. I am not changing it."

"If you don't ease up on the policy, then you're going to lose their business!"

"I'm not going to change the closing policy. She can go somewhere else to shop if she doesn't like it."

"You know, all day you've been upsetting me," my mother yelled. "You don't want to pay for my parking tickets. Fine! I can pay for my own stuff. But running the store the way you do is becoming a pain in everyone's ass."

"Ms. Brown, I don't want to talk about this anymore with you," I said, trying to remain calm. "I'm not changing the closing policy, and that's final. I'm tired of arguing about the same thing every day. I just want to go home and relax."

"Charm, you're a fucking bitch."

It sounded like Ms. Brown had just retched through the phone, and I got caught in the spewing. It was that loud and guttural voice I was all too familiar with since I landed in this country. I hung up the phone while she was still screaming.

I was livid and almost paralyzed by what she had called me. Memories I hadn't thought about in years flooded my space. I needed relief and almost evoked my childhood reverie of being adopted to protect myself from those terrible memories and Ms. Brown's menacing behavior.

But not this time. Ms. Brown's statement was a jolt into a new awareness: *I deserve better.* Ms. Brown had been pounding on my self-esteem since I had landed in this country. This was the last time I was going to endure her calling me names.

When I arrived home, my children were asleep, and Marlon had settled into bed. I was relieved because I had no strength to pretend everything was fine with me. I hoped a shower would bring more relief. I changed the spray settings to the highest power massage, closed my eyes, and stood with the water beating down on my head to wash away the day's troubles. I wanted to wash away the dysfunctional relationship I had with Ms. Brown. The shower helped a little but wasn't enough. I crawled into bed next to Marlon hoping to fall asleep immediately.

I kept hearing Ms. Brown's words over and over again in my head, "*Charm, you're a fucking bitch.*" I couldn't shake the anger that was boiling inside of me. Even though I was exhausted from the day, I felt a strong urge to read the book sitting on my night-stand, *Messages from the Masters* by Brian Weiss.

I grabbed the book and went to the living room. When I opened it, this was what I saw:

Sometimes your biological family is not your real
family. Your parents, your siblings, and your
other relatives may not understand you. They
may not express love and caring to you.
They may reject you and treat you cruelly. You
are not obligated to be treated inhumanely. There
is no karmic responsibility that is met by being a
target for the abusive behavior of others, family
or not. To abuse or to harm someone is an act of
choice or free will by the abuser. Abuse is *never*
deserved.

As you grow older, you may find yourself
surrounded by friends and others who genuinely
care for you, who provide the security that comes
from being loved and treated with dignity and
respect. These friends and loved ones become
your true family. They may share your spiritual
values, too, and you may help each other evolve
in a positive way. These people are your spiritual
family.

I had allowed Ms. Brown to continue to verbally abuse me as
an adult. I was no longer a helpless child, and I wanted it to stop.
When you've been brainwashed your whole life to respect your
parents regardless of their actions towards you, it is not easy to find
the power to change a pattern of abuse. I understood after reading
that passage that this challenge was part of my soul work and I
was ready to surmount it.

I've questioned the meaning of family after experiencing my
family's deceit and lack of care for me growing up. Brian Weiss'
words supported a personal belief that I kept from everyone, that
my biological family was not my real family. No wonder I fantasized about being adopted. My belief was reinforced by their lack
of generosity towards me when I was homeless. We tend to excuse
family members for their cruel actions towards us because we are

related by blood. But we shouldn't. We are not obligated to endure cruelty. Who we choose as our family is entirely up to us. We are not bonded by blood. Redefining the meaning of family may be an uncommon way to think, but I finally knew that honoring my own personal belief was more important than honoring a family that had not served me well.

I had denied what Ms. Brown had done to me. She picked on me. She bullied me. She reduced me to a mere shadow of my greatest potential with her words and actions. Abuse is something we're never supposed to talk about, as Grandma said, but that must change for our future generations to thrive. My true feelings about Ms. Brown showed in my responses to her or lack thereof. It showed in our disputes. And it showed in our coldness towards each other.

Ms. Brown's profane words still bothered me, so I trudged down the stairs to our family room to meditate. I sat on the floor with my back against the sofa and my legs crossed. I needed to be honest about what had happened in my childhood. I needed to face the memories I'd consciously suppressed and ignored. They controlled my life, and I desired freedom. Freedom from the unsettling memories and this unhealthy relationship. I didn't know where I was going with this, but I made a conscious decision to not allow them to live inside of me anymore.

I closed my eyes, breathed slowly, and readied myself to look at the situations in my childhood that haunted me.

CHAPTER TEN

A Guided Visitation to Remember the Past

"Until you make the unconscious conscious, it will direct your life and you will call it fate." This quote by Carl Jung popped into my head while I took deep breaths in and out. I could feel my hesitancy by the uneasiness in my stomach, but I continued with the intention of visiting my most difficult memories. The ones that sporadically show up at the most inopportune times to remind me that something was still unresolved. I thought about my trip to South Africa and discussing Nelson Mandela and the "Invictus" poem with fellow safarians. Would I continue to allow my life to be directed by fate or did I want to be the master of my fate, the captain of my soul? *I am the master of my fate. I am the master of my fate.* I repeated it in my mind.

I pictured myself sitting on the cloud with my feet dangling, but this time it wasn't ten-year-old Charm sitting there, it was the current version of me. I wasn't going to look for my fantasized family but face my childhood where my trauma originated. With my laser beam eyesight, I found our home at 1131 Ogden Avenue. I swooped down and entered the door to apartment 16F. Our three-bedroom apartment had two bathrooms, living and dining rooms, a kitchen, and wall-to-wall windows, with a large terrace the length of the apartment. My programmed perception of happiness began here.

I proceed hesitantly down the hall to my old bedroom. I linger by the door preparing for whatever might present itself. Taking a deep breath and a tentative step forward, I cross the threshold into the trauma space of my childhood. On the surface, my bedroom is ready for the arrival of a princess. It's beautifully decorated in pink and white. The walls are covered in a pink-and-white checkered glossy wallpaper, lined with a pink border engraved with flowers. Pink curtains cover my large double window. My twin-size canopy bed has a pink-and-white checkered bedspread with a matching bed skirt. Half my bed is filled with stuffed animals. A wooden desk sits near the window hosting a pink-and-white desk pad, a pink pencil cup holder, a writing pad, and pencils. My large closet is filled with more dresses and shoes than pants and sneakers.

A toy box sits in a corner of the room overflowing with toys. I love toys but love books even more. I own only one, *The Secret Garden*, a present from Aunt Steph when I left for America. She wrapped it in a brown paper bag and instructed me to open it when I landed. Underneath my bed, hidden by the long bed skirt, is a flashlight and the novel *It's Not the End of the World* by my favorite author, Judy Blume. I borrowed it from the school library. This is my refuge. My hiding place where I feel safe. My own private island that no one knows exists.

I look at my bay window and see my brothers and I jumping in and out of the windows of the bedrooms onto the terrace, playing tag. I recall sitting on the windowsill looking out at the moon at night or laying on my stomach with my ankles crossed in the air reading. How could a room so beautiful hold an abundance of unhappy memories within its walls?

I turn my attention to my bed and see Charm at ten years old. She has all the earthly things that she'll ever want and need, yet

Charm lies there in tears as her emotional state weakens from her mother's abuse, her insides bound together by unexpressed emotions and a quieted voice. I see a slow, agonizing death of her spirit, plagued with sadness. She doesn't feel safe or loved or wanted.

What can be done for her now as I stand in the doorway of my early life, pondering how to help Charm? I walk towards her almost diminished light and crawl in bed next to her and hold her for a while. Words come to me that will seed a full poem years later. *She needed beauty. Again. She needed a gentle caress. Again. She needed love. Again.*

"You're not alone," I whisper to Charm. "I am here now."

A shard of memory floats towards us, one I tried to bury so often, but it rears its head to say it still exists within me:

Charm is cleaning. Charm's always cleaning. By the time she was nine years old, she was the full-time caregiver, babysitter, and tutor for her brothers, plus Ms. Brown's housekeeper, nail technician, and part-time cook. It's Friday evening. Adrian, Brian, and Charm can play outside until 8 p.m. since it's not a school night, but chores must be done before Ms. Brown arrives home from work around 9 p.m. Charm chooses to do chores before going out to play, knowing she will have a difficult time getting Adrian and Brian to return home in time for her to finish all the housework.

After arriving home from school at 3:15 p.m., Charm makes peanut butter and jelly sandwiches for her brothers, pours their favorite fruit punch in their Batman cups, and turns on the television so they can watch Batman and Robin. She wolfs down a few graham crackers before changing out of her school clothes, then goes about the business of cleaning Ms. Brown's apartment.

She always starts with her parents' bedroom at the far end of the apartment. Ms. Brown didn't make her bed that morning. *Ugh!* Charm thinks. *More work for me to do.* She makes her parents' bed, hangs up her father's shirts, puts Ms. Brown's nightgown in their laundry basket, and dusts the furniture.

Next, she peeks into her room to admire it. It's spotless. Charm cleaned it last night when everyone else was asleep to save time on Friday. Plus, her room is usually tidy. Charm moves onto her brother's room. Her smile quickly changes to a frown. *What a mess!* She picks up their filthy underwear off the floor, dresser, table, and chairs. She makes their beds. Puts away their toys and dusts their furniture. Then, she lays out their play clothes.

Life is unfair, Charm screams inward. *If Adrian and Brian were taught to be responsible for their own room, I wouldn't have so much to do.* Charm is incensed by their lack of responsibility and being taken advantage of. *They are almost eight years old. They can take care of themselves.*

Next, the two bathrooms. First, the green one. All accessories are green. Ms. Brown loves green. This room will take longer because it is the full bath. Charm changes all the towels and empties the built-in hamper. Cleanse the tub, sink, and toilet. "Charm, hurry up. We want to go outside to play!" shouts Brian.

"A little while longer," Charm shouts back. Next, the pink bathroom, the half bath. She changes all the towels, empties the built-in hamper, cleans the sink and toilet. She must use a lot of ammonia and Ajax because if the bathrooms don't smell like cleaning products, she'll be in trouble with Ms. Brown.

Now, for the living room. She turns off the television. "Oh man!" Adrian says, "it's not finished, turn it back on!"

"No!" Charm replies. "This is a rerun anyway."

Charm states a stream of instructions to her brothers. "Put your dishes in the sink, please. Go wash your hands and face. Change out of your school clothes and put them on top of the laundry basket, then put on the clothes I left on the bed. I'll clean the living room in the meantime."

Adrian and Brian sigh, stand up, and storm off to do as they are told.

Charm cleans her father's component stereo set. She dusts the center table, then the two end tables, the large television, and on top of the VCR. She hates dusting the bookcases because she has to take down the family's *World Book Encyclopedias* and the *Childcraft* books sets and dust them one by one. Any other day, she would love to dust them individually but not today. No one else in the house reads them but her. She loves playing school with her brothers and doing the experiments in the *Childcraft* book set. When she is done, she fluffs the pillows.

"Make sure your room is the way I left it!" she shouts at her brothers, "Else we are not going outside to play."

She giggles as she hears their moans and groans. Adrian and Brian start to argue, and she hears banging noises coming from the room.

"If that room is messed up, we are not going outside today. I mean it!" she shouts. She turns the television back on and goes to the dining room.

"Ok, we're ready," says Brian.

"I'm almost done," Charm replies.

"You always have so much to do!"

"Not my fault. Go get our bikes from the terrace and put them in the hallway outside the door. Then sit in the living room until it's time to go."

The dining room, for the most part, is pretty clean. Charm does certain chores during the week so it doesn't take up so much time on Fridays. For instance, she cleans the dining room cabinet by taking out every piece of china, washing them, and cleaning the glass with newspaper and water. Using newspaper instead of a window cleaner makes the cabinet glass sparkle and doesn't leave streaks. Her mother taught her that. She wipes the plastic covers of the dining room chairs, pushing them all back to make sure they all line up.

Finally, the last leg of the cleaning tour—Ms. Brown's Kitchen. Charm changes all the dish cloths and towels and throws the dirty ones on the chair in the living room. She loads the dishwasher with the breakfast dishes and starts it. She washes the pots and pan, cleans the stove, and wipes the counters and kitchen table.

"Adrian and Brian, what do you want for dinner?" she shouts out to her brothers. "There is chicken pot pie, hamburgers and fries, hotdogs, or I could make corned beef and rice."

Her brothers interrupt in unison, "Burgers and fries."

She takes out the pack of ground beef already made into burgers from the freezer, seasons one side with garlic powder, seasoned salt, and black pepper, then flips them over and repeats. She puts them in the refrigerator. She puts the garbage bin in the hallway, then sweeps and mops the floor.

Charm picks up the kitchen towels off the chair in the living room and prepares for wash day tomorrow. She empties her parents' hamper at the end of the hall. She pours her own on top of her parents' and empties her brothers' basket on top of all the other dirty clothes in the hallway. Next, she separates everything onto the floor and puts each load one by one back in the laundry basket.

She can hear her brothers getting restless. They begin arguing again.

"I'm almost done," she shouts to them.

She retrieves the vacuum cleaner from the hallway closet and begins vacuuming from her parents' bedroom and throughout the whole house.

When she's done, Charm snatches her watch off her dresser and puts it on to keep track of time. Wrestling the house keys from the key rack, she says, "Let's go, I'm ready now."

"Finally!" say Adrian and Brian.

She double-locks the front door and they grab their bikes and race downstairs. It is now 4:45 p.m.

Through this minute-by-minute replay I'm guiding myself through, I feel Charm's overwhelm, her overly responsible nature forming, and her deep fear of disappointing Ms. Brown. She loved her brothers but wanted to remove them from her hips. They'd been there for as long as she could remember. They were getting too big to carry. She wanted to be free of so much responsibility.

To continue helping Charm, I have to look at each memory head-on. No more turning away as I felt each one. I'm reliving my childhood from a more aware and truthful place, not from Charm's perspective. The true perspective is that my abuse was not my fault,

They return upstairs by 7:30 p.m. so Charm can make dinner. She tells her brothers to put the bikes on the terrace and to wash their hands. She turns on the television and goes to the kitchen to prepare snacks for Adrian and Brian. She puts the hamburgers in the toaster broiler and the fries in the oven. She washes a small pot of rice and puts it on top of the stove. She plans to make the corned beef and rice for her parents' dinner. When the rice comes to a boil, she adds salt and a quarter stick of butter, turns the stove down low, and leaves it to cook.

She gives her brothers each a Twinkie and a cup of water to snack on, using disposable dinnerware, while they watch television until dinner is ready. "Can we have lemonade for dinner?" asks Brian.

"Sure," Charm replies. She flips the burgers. Then, she slices up a small onion for the burgers. She opens the broiler and puts the onions on top of the hamburgers. She makes the lemonade, fetches three glasses, puts ice cubes in them, and sets them aside. She cuts up another small onion, green bell peppers, and tomatoes for the corned beef and sets those ingredients aside. Then, she toasts the hamburger bread in the toaster and puts mayonnaise on her brothers' bread only. Charm hates mayonnaise. She adds lettuce and tomatoes to the top of the bread.

"When will dinner be ready, Charmie? I'm starving," asks Adrian. The timer on the broiler says two more minutes.

"Two minutes," she shouts back. She pours the lemonade in the plastic cups and puts them around the dining room table. She gets three paper plates from the cabinet and lays them out on the counter. She takes out the fries from the oven and dishes them out evenly on the plates with the burger rolls. She takes the burgers from the broiler and puts them on the buns. She adds ketchup to the burgers only, because they all like different variations of ketchup on their fries. She knows Adrian will pour ketchup all over his fries while Brian will pour ketchup on the side of his plate to dip his fries in it. Charm pours a small amount of ketchup on her fries.

She puts the plates around the dining room table and calls her brothers for dinner. "Make sure you throw your snack plates and cups in the garbage."

Her brothers do as Charm tells them and sit down to eat while Charm goes to the living room to make sure they didn't leave any crumbs or garbage behind. She turns off the stove and sets the pot of rice on the back burner. Then she sits in the dining room with her brothers and eats. She rushes to chew so she can finish making dinner for her parents.

She puts the small, Jamaican Dutch pot on the stove, adds a tablespoon of oil, and turns on the stove. She grabs the vegetables she prepared earlier as seasoning and adds them to the hot oil. She stirs the seasoning around, covers the pot, and turns down the stove. Then, she opens a can of corned beef, adds it to the pot along with a small amount of black pepper and a slice of scotch bonnet pepper. She smashes the corned beef in the pot and covers it.

Charm takes her plate from the table and throws it in the garbage. She gulps down her lemonade and finishes making her parents' meal.

Her father arrives home and greets them. He dishes himself some of the corned beef and rice, grabs a beer, and says, "Thank you, my daughter."

"You're welcome, Daddy," Charm says as he sits down in front of the television.

When they are done eating, Adrian and Brian put the disposables in the garbage. Charm wipes the dining room mats, pushes the chairs, wipes the counter and the stove. She cleans the broiler toaster and goes to her room. Adrian and Brian go to their room to play.

Ms. Brown arrives at 8:58 p.m.

Charm becomes stultified by Ms. Brown's presence in the apartment. Her heart flutters, anticipating some kind of punishment when Ms. Brown walks past her bedroom and does not acknowledge her. Ms. Brown goes to her room, changes out of her working attire, then walks to the living room in her usual disputatious manner.

"Charm, come here," she shouts harshly.

Charm's heart pounds at this familiar tone. It portends a slap for something Ms. Brown is not pleased with. *What could possibly be wrong?* she thinks to herself. She begins double-checking in her mind what she might have forgotten to do as she drags herself to the living room.

"Yes, Mom," she says, standing far out of reach of Ms. Brown's hands.

But Ms. Brown doesn't buy it. "Come here!"

Ms. Brown wants her in reach for what comes next. Charm walks slowly towards her irascible mother, and as soon as she is within reach, Ms. Brown slaps her across the face. Hard.

Charm holds her hand to her jaw and cries silently.

"Did you dust on top of the television?" Ms. Brown barks.

"I did," Charm says in a quivering voice.

Ms. Brown does the finger test on the one spot Charm missed, the spot under the VCR. Charm forgot to move the VCR.

"If you dusted it well, then I shouldn't have dust on my finger. Get the cloth and furniture polish and dust the television again!"

Charm's father looks up from the television and confronts his wife.

"Fay, was that necessary? The house is immaculate, and she made dinner."

It is one of the few times her father shows care for her. He usually just grimaces to avoid arguing with Ms. Brown.

Ms. Brown sucks her teeth and says, "I don't care. She must learn to clean properly and thoroughly. There should be no dust anywhere. I don't want my allergies to bother me tonight."

Her father shakes his head and goes back to watching the boxing match with a grimace on his face.

Charm re-dusts the television and VCR as she holds back tears of humiliation. She scurries to her bedroom when she is done, hoping to avoid any more of Ms. Brown's wrath. She sits on her bedroom floor with her back to her bed. Her life feels like a perpetual nightmare. She grabs a pillow from her bed and lays on her pink carpet. She wipes away her tears and invokes her super-hero reverie to salve her wounds and disheartened spirit. It is all she can do to ease her pain momentarily.

Even though Charm was crying, I could feel my own adult anger rising fast. Deep down Charm despised her own mother. But she would never let anyone know it. She held everything within. She had no one to help her process her life and no embodied horizons nearby to remind her of who she really was, so anger grew within instead of love.

Charm arouses from her reverie but doesn't notice that her mother has put her nursing shoes in her doorway along with the Holly-wood Sani-White All-White shoe polish to conceal the scuff marks. This is another one of Charm's jobs. She has to whiten all of her mother's nursing shoes for work. She doesn't know Ms. Brown was initially off from work but was called in last minute.

Charm turns off her lamp light and crawls into bed. Moments later, she is awakened by her mother yelling and shaking her.

"Charm, you didn't whiten my goddamn shoes, and I am running late. Get the hell up and do it now!"

Charm rises as quickly as she can, jumps to her feet, and begins whitening Ms. Brown's shoes. With her eyes glazed over from being woken abruptly, she mistakenly gets whitening on the heel of one shoe and doesn't notice. She puts the shoes near her mother's doorway and goes back to sleep.

She is awakened again with Ms. Brown now screaming in her face.

"This is a sloppy job you did. There's polish on the heel of my shoes."

Ms. Brown pulls her arm.

"Get up, wet a rag, and wipe off the heel. I can't go to work looking sloppy. You don't do anything with care," she yells as she throws the shoe on the floor.

Charm gets up, takes her mother's nursing shoe and staggers to the bathroom. She douses her face with water to wake herself up, then wipes her face with one of the face towels. She pulls one of the disposable cloths from cabinet underneath the sink in the green bathroom, wets it with water, and begins wiping the heel of Ms. Brown's shoes. Ms. Brown is still carrying on.

"Sometimes, you're just a worthless piece of shit. Now I am late for work because of you."

Charm is not the reason she is late for work. Ms. Brown is chronically tardy. She would be late whether or not her shoes were cleaned correctly from the night before.

When Ms. Brown leaves for work, Charm can't go back to sleep, so she reaches for her blanket and a pillow and goes underneath her bed. She picks up a flashlight and *Are You There God? It's Me, Margaret* by Judy Blume that she has just started.

Charm often gets into trouble for reading. Chores are more important. That's just the way it is in her household, so she rarely has time to indulge herself. She should always be doing something around the house or taking care of her brothers instead. She isn't allowed to read late at night either because she should be sleeping, even if there is no school tomorrow. So, she goes underneath her bed where books are hidden when she thinks everyone is asleep.

Charm reads until about two in the morning.

She wakes up the next morning around 8 a.m. Her brothers are hungry, and her parents are still asleep. Her father had picked up her mother from Parkview Nursing Home where she worked from 11 p.m. to 7 a.m. *Then they'll both sleep until late. It's laundry day,* she thinks to herself.

I can feel how exhausted Charm was from that day and her entire life. Her life was a routine of caring for others without concern for her own desires. The only desire I sense that she had was getting the hell away from this household and never returning.

First, she must tend to Adrian and Brian then get the laundry done alone. She has eight loads to do today. She tells her brothers to brush their teeth and wash their faces. Charm brushes her teeth, then goes into the kitchen to make them eggs, bacon, and plantains. She pours the frozen orange juice from the container into the jug, adding water and sugar to sweeten it. The three of them sit in the living room to watch Bugs Bunny and eat breakfast.

When they are done, she cleans the kitchen and then gets dressed. Charm puts the detergent, bleach, and fabric softener in the cart. She takes her Judy Blume book and the roll of quarters from the tray in the living room. Telling Adrian and Brian to keep it down because their parents are still asleep, she heads out the door to do the family's laundry.

On the elevator, Charm presses B for basement. The elevator stops on the fourteenth floor, and an older lady gets on and presses L for lobby.

"Young lady, I see you almost every week going to do laundry by yourself. How old are you?" the lady says.

"I'm nine."

"Where's your mother?"

"Asleep."

"And you do your family's laundry all by yourself at your age?"

Charm nods yes. The lady doesn't know that Charm has been doing the laundry by herself since she was about eight years old.

"Your mother feels comfortable with you in the basement of an apartment building all by yourself?"

Charm shrugs. She's not really into having this conversation. It doesn't make her feel good inside. It is bringing up a lot of fear that she has about being in that basement by herself.

Every now and then Charms sees friends ambling through the basement to the other side of the building to visit friends. They laugh at Charm and call her an old lady or maid. Charm never sees any one of her friends in the basement doing their family's laundry.

This day, the laundromat in the building is closed, so Charm has to walk three blocks to the public laundromat. She feels so embarrassed walking up the street with a cart full of clothes to wash. She prays that she won't see her friends, so they won't make fun of her and tell everyone in school later.

By the time Charm arrives home from doing the laundry, her parents are out food shopping. She has to clean the kitchen again after Ms. Brown made breakfast for herself and her husband. Ms. Brown doesn't clean up much after herself because she has Charm.

Charm puts away everyone's clothes. By this time, her parents are back. Charm has to put away all of the groceries and help Ms. Brown prepare for lunch and dinner because they are eating in. Charm cleans the kitchen after each meal as well. Adrian and Brian never have to do chores. Her brothers are never asked to help out in the kitchen or put away groceries. They don't clean their own rooms.

When I came from Jamaica to live with my parents, so much was expected of me and only me. I often felt like Ms. Brown's slave. I felt like a stepdaughter instead of her daughter. This further created distance between us. Who I had become by my early teens was based on my early associations, primarily the dysfunctional relationship I had with my parents, especially my mother.

I hold Charm with love and weep with her. I speak to her as lovingly as possible.

"You are no longer responsible for this burden. I won't allow this to go on any further," I reassure her.

"Give me all your woes," I beg. "I can take them now. I am strong enough to take the reins."

I promise her I will continue on to free our soul. We both need to be free of the chains imposed by Ms. Brown and her constant reinforcements of generational patterns.

I committed once a week to sit with young Charm. Even more often, if suppressed memories surfaced without warning. I'd cry, or quiver, or my heart would race when I was done. I cursed Ms. Brown in my mind, vowing never to see or talk to her again (although that wasn't yet practical). I welcomed all honest feelings towards her. Truth made me win more and more battles, and Ms. Brown was close to losing this generational war.

One morning when I was alone in my house, I said out loud, "I don't like my mother." Then I shouted it into the atmosphere. Then I screamed it. I kept on screaming. Afterwards, I felt better. The stigma of saying that about my mother was loosening, and I was starting to care less about what people might think of me.

These guided visitations to my past were Charm and Kadian's harbinger of hope to co-create a greater version possible of each other. I realized how deep in obligation I stood with Ms. Brown. And sensed how my insides were wracked with the guilt of disappointing Ms. Brown. I got more honest with my past and braver to face it with each personal session I gave myself.

I was beginning to feel less obligation to Ms. Brown, indicating Charm was untethering herself from the reality where she had been stuck. Charm was growing and expanding and would soon merge with the parts of her that carried on while she was spiritually comatose. I knew she would join me soon at our latest potential.

CHAPTER ELEVEN
The Year of Honesty

My guided meditations helped me to become more courageous in my life. It wasn't just about facing my past abuse or standing up to Ms. Brown, but I was becoming brave enough to follow my horizon. I would no longer be postponing my happiness for anyone, not even my children. My role in their lives is to be their embodied horizon, not to cower in fear of creating the life I want to exist in. True bravery is following your horizon. I want them to be brave enough to be who they really are in this world.

Most people around me did not understand about energy healing, but I loved unconventional medicine, and no one was going to deter me from it any longer. I went to Washington for my first intuitive energy healing session with Marie in January 2010, despite what anyone might have thought. I hopped on Marie's table with excitement, ready to hear all about this new life I was in the midst of creating. Prior to the appointment, I wrote down fifteen questions pertaining to a career change, intuition, weight, and possibly relocating. But as I laid on her table, it felt as if my own energy had betrayed me.

I was not prepared to talk about Ms. Brown, but Marie zoned in on my mother immediately. "Your mother's a habitual liar."

She read my past as if my energy handed her a manual to recite from. It felt like I was having invasive surgery as she interpreted my life accurately, but it also felt like someone was walking in my shoes for a moment. She concluded the talk about my mother by saying I needed to get away from her *now*. She confirmed the realization I had come to myself by the end of 2009.

Marie told me about her program where she mentored people in energy, energy medicine, intuition, and personal growth. So I applied, once again on faith, not knowing the hows and whys, and I was accepted for the 2011 class. This program was monthly for one year and 2,400 miles away. I wondered how I would be able to do this financially, given we'd be down to one income when I closed my last retail store at the end of March. My intuition told me to call my safari roommate and ask if I could stay with her on my monthly trips. Being vulnerable, especially when it comes to asking for help, is not my strong suit, and it took a lot of courage and strength to ask, but I did. She said, "Of course." Our meeting in South Africa was not a coincidence but synchronicity showing off when I stepped onto this path wholeheartedly.

Marie and I discussed creating healthy changes within me and to see myself as an individual. I left the session feeling emotionally healthier. The argument in December 2009 with Ms. Brown had forced me to look at my emotional traumas with honest eyes. My energy healing session enforced that my theme for 2010 would be "the year of honesty." I would feel shifts occurring inward for many months after as I continued with my journaling and now my self-guided visualizations of my childhood. No more pretending and repressing. No more pleasing others and leaving myself out of my decisions going forward.

I was still in Washington when I received an irate phone call from my employee. She had gotten into an argument with Ms. Brown, who as usual became extremely disrespectful. My employee said,

"I will not tolerate Ms. Brown speaking to me the way Ms. Brown speaks to you."

I could feel my small self in her words. *Why did I continue to tolerate this abuse?* I felt ashamed, weak, and underdeveloped. The contrast between who I was fighting to be and who I was in Ms. Brown's company were like fire and water. She doused my light at every opportunity. I knew what I had to do, but what was stopping me from doing it? With only two months left on my lease, I had to take action so that the remaining time would be peaceful for myself and my employee. I could no longer put Ms. Brown's daily living expenses ahead of my emotional health. Besides, she was not being honest about her finances. She was more than capable of maintaining the lifestyle she wanted without a paycheck from me. I was fed up with her lies and manipulation. For more than four decades, I'd nurtured everybody instead of myself. I'd adhered to everyone else's opinion. I'd put everyone else first. I had to choose myself in this situation or die spiritually.

After the phone call, I laid in bed for a long time talking to God. Then I meditated. I put my right hand on my second chakra and my left hand on my third and took deep breaths in and out. Tears fell immediately because I had had enough. I focused on my breath, and within minutes, I felt myself connecting. My feelings of frustration were gone, and my reality disappeared.

I opened my internal eye and realized I was sitting on a bench in front of a body of water. This place was unfamiliar to me. There was an array of beautiful flowers with different colors all around this body of water. I saw trees everywhere, but they didn't look normal. At a closer glance, I noticed their branches were frozen and turned to ice, as if it should have been extremely cold where I was sitting. It seemed peculiar, given I didn't feel cold, flowers were blooming all around, and the body of water was flowing instead of iced over. It was beautiful, nonetheless. I heard footsteps approaching, and I turned towards the sound.

It was Ms. Brown. Wearing all-white attire, she looked beautiful and angelic. She stopped a few feet from where I was sitting, put her hand on her chest, and said, "Forgive me. I don't remember who I really am." Then she patted her heart and walked away. I watched her until she disappeared into the field of icy trees.

When I came out of the meditation I was drenched in tears. I got out of bed and went to the bathroom to brush my teeth. When I looked in the mirror, I saw that image of her mouthing those words to me.

"Forgive me. I don't remember who I really am."

I whispered back, "I'm trying, but you are not making it easy for me." Then I got ready and departed for the airport.

On the plane, I asked myself that question again, "What am I willing to risk?" I had to risk what society might think of me if I made the choice to remove my own mother from my life. I had to risk one of us leaving this planet and never resolving our issues. My own happiness and health were far more important than staying in a tumultuous relationship that did not serve me. Looking at my mother's and my grandmother's relationship put things into further perspective for me. I didn't want my children and I to continue this pattern of mistreating each other. Changing familial patterns was of utmost importance to me now, and I was willing to eradicate this pattern even without Ms. Brown's help. I was ready.

The night I arrived home from Washington, I sat in my living room and journaled. That fear of what society might think of me or my children not having a grandmother in their lives—a fear that had anchored me for so long—melted away and its pathway imploded. My readiness and what I was willing to chance steadied my gait on this new course that had begun on the plane to South Africa. And I now felt courageous enough to continue on.

When I finished journaling, I closed my eyes and conversed with the God I've come to know. I didn't bark demands or harbor any resentment from unfilled expectations, as when I was a child. I didn't have expectations of God, who certainly didn't expect anything from me. God is the light. A beacon when I'm lost. The memory of my light. The essence of my soul. There's never a reason to come and get me out of the darkness, for God's special light exists everywhere. I can see it from anywhere. God is the horizon.

My conversation with God ceased. And there was nothing. No sound, as if I had suddenly lost my hearing. No heaviness, like my body had fallen away. What was left of me began free falling. I couldn't see a beginning. There was no end. Then a mere aperture appeared and I was pulled towards its opening. I orbited in that place briefly and felt a recalibration of my energy. It's that place where no human can go physically. Where clarity and certainty exist. Where Love is pronounced. It's where my soul waits patiently for me to become responsive.

Moments later, I could feel my body again. I opened my eyes and felt an inner stirring that I've never felt before.

I finally understood inspiration. Inspiration is the beckoning call of your soul. Turning towards the beckoning begins the work to reacquaint you again.

There was no turning back for me now. Every experience in my life was helping me to understand the process, and with understanding comes trust. When you trust the process, you trust life, and then you can truly say you trust God. I was finally trusting the process.

I traveled to New York early the next day. I wanted to confront Ms. Brown before opening of the business day. When I arrived, my employee was counting inventory, Grandma was sitting in her favorite spot, and Ms. Brown sat in my office having breakfast.

I said good morning to my employee and Grandma only. I stood at the doorway of my office and confronted Ms. Brown.

"When are you going to learn how to respect others around you?" I asked. She knew exactly what I was talking about because she didn't ask me to clarify anything.

Ms. Brown sucked her teeth and said, "Oh, please. Don't tell me what to do."

"I've had enough of you. I would like you to leave now."

"You don't tell me what to do!" Ms. Brown shouted.

"Okay, Charm," Grandma interjected. "I know you're upset, but that is the past. Let it go."

I ignored my grandmother and, in a harsh, cold, and loud voice, I shouted at Ms. Brown, "Get the hell out of my store now. You don't own anything here, and you are not in charge of anything here. Get your ass up, and get the hell out. Do not come back into my store ever again."

Ms. Brown gathered up her belongings as quickly as she could, exited my office, and paced nervously back and forth. I waited for the cantankerous spirit that had inhabited my mother's body to take charge once more. It didn't take long.

"You're a piece of shit." She never fails to show up. I didn't react, for I was trying to break this generational pattern. Then she turned to Grandma and said, "Let's go, Ma. She doesn't want us here. Let's get the hell out of her store."

"She didn't ask me to leave, she asked you," replied Grandma. "But I'll go with you."

"Grandma, you are welcome here anytime, but your daughter is not," I said.

I will not write all the terrible things Ms. Brown said to me that day, but know that I kept my composure. Every step she took towards the entrance of my store, she told me exactly how she felt about me, and it's not worth repeating. I knew she wasn't going to leave peacefully, but I wasn't going to back down. Every step she took closer to the entrance, I kept envisioning her as the person in my meditation. If only she could remember who she really was at

the core. But when Ms. Brown left, the air of contempt left with
her. I heard my employee breathe a sigh of relief.

On the drive home, the middle of my forehead started throbbing. I
recognized Brian's presence. I had felt him often since his death
and had come to know when he was around me. He showed up at
times like this to console my sadness, quell my fears, or encourage
me to stand up to Ms. Brown. "Charm, you are healing the dead,
the living, and the unborn. Thank you for doing what I couldn't do
for myself. Keep going."

Brian's words gave me a broader perspective on my soul work. I
was healing beyond myself—healing my family, past, present and
future. It made me braver. Brian's words also emboldened me to
disengage from Ms. Brown. If we were together, such as attending
a family function, and she started with her pattern of talking to me
in a harsh tone or raising her voice, I would drive off and not call
her later. I no longer entertained her outbursts. If we were on the
phone and she started yelling, I hung up on her. Before, I would
wait a few days and call her, trying to be the daughter she expected
of me; then we both pretended as if it hadn't happened. No more
of those phone calls were made.

On March 31, 2010, I closed my second store. I felt an exorbitant
amount of relief leaving that life behind. Authentic happiness
exuded from me like in South Africa. I drove the entire way
home smiling with a sense of accomplishment. I was finally free.
Free of a business I was not passionate about and mostly free of
Ms. Brown. I decided not to attend any more family functions or
holiday gatherings. No more conversations over the phone either.
I wanted to dismantle other family obligations. I wouldn't be
returning to New York for a while. The break would be easy since
Ms. Brown and I weren't on speaking terms anyway. It was
important to make room for my emotional healing and to focus

on the process of forgiveness because it doesn't happen overnight.

Sometimes I still wonder, if my mother had understood the effects of her damaging words on me, would the abuse have ended right then? If she felt empathy, would she have taken me in her arms and said, "I will never hurt you again"? I wonder. If I could have seen that hurting child within her, would I have harbored anger towards her as an adult? If I could have heard my mother's higher self say during the abuse, "Forgive me, child. I've forgotten who I am because I am disconnected from my true nature," would I have understood her erratic behavior? I wonder. My mother was an unloved and unconscious being. And she, too, was modified and had lost connection with her soul.

Ms. Brown tried to contact me during my sabbatical. I did not answer any of her calls. She called Marlon to get a hold of me, but I refused to talk to her. My decision was final, and I told Marlon to tell her that I did not want to speak to her or want to see her for a while or maybe ever again. She didn't call me for months.

My mental, emotional, and physical health improved with no engagement with Ms. Brown. For years, our situation made me depressed and gave me a backache that wouldn't go away. Our contentious relationship harmed my spirit. I shrunk every time her phone number lit up my phone. Everything was improving for me. So, I stuck to the choices I made because they were working on my behalf. To break our generational pattern, I had to choose differently than Ms. Brown would have in this situation. She would never have reduced or severed interactions with her own mother and family. They will forever be enmeshed in their dysfunction.

I knew I was on the right track because I was guilt-free with what I had chosen to do. I ceased pushing my emotions down or aside no matter how they hurt when I faced them. I continued my visualization of looking honestly at my past, feeling my emotions until they waned. I wasn't expecting to eradicate the pain or any patterns immediately. I knew they would diminish over time with less impact on my life.

. . .

Distancing myself from Ms. Brown and her side of the family was a gigantic leap to eradicating generational patterns, but I had other relationships to terminate. My vow to eliminate what was not conducive to my happiness encouraged me to take an honest assessment of others in my life as well. I started to see traits of my mother in other relationships.

One day, in the middle of a disagreement with a friend, she became caustic and disrespectful. She resorted to calling me names and making assumptions. In that moment, I realized I was arguing with Ms. Brown again. I had to be honest with myself about the discreet signs that had been showing up over the course of this two-year relationship.

I knew from experience with Ms. Brown that trying to make relationships work and staying the same course when others are unwilling to grow would deter my happiness. This person had many characteristics I had grown to love but there were a few I just couldn't live with. In the moment of my friend's rageful behavior, that awareness gave me the opportunity months later to choose once again. Was I going to pick my mother or myself? It was an easy choice, and I abruptly ended our friendship. My path to authentic happiness and to my soul was more important.

Even though my friend apologized repeatedly and tried to rekindle our friendship, my answer remained the same. Ms. Brown had not changed enough for us to move past what happened and for it not to happen again. I wasn't inviting any more relations in my life where it mimicked the relationship I had with Ms. Brown —harsh, disrespectful, and dysfunctional. When I made that connection, it was a done deal for me.

The ending of that relationship shoved me down my happiness path, and I slammed into one of my deepest fears. I had to become braver and more willing to risk than I'd ever been before. I had to address that thing I've been avoiding since my twenties: my marriage of twenty-one years. This was the relationship where I could have garnered an Oscar nomination for the best pretending leading lady.

My family and friends viewed my life like a happy television sitcom. I had a faithful, devoted, kind, and financially supportive husband. He wasn't verbally, emotionally, or physically abusive. This was different from what most women in my family and friends experienced in their relationships. Someone else's life may appear to be what you think you want on the surface but might not be conducive to your own personal happiness. In my own sitcom, like Truman, I was unhappy despite everything I had. I had to take off my mask to face the real me.

Marlon deeply loved me, and I loved him, but I was in a marriage with no depth, and I am a deep person. Marlon didn't have the capacity to go there with me. It was obvious from the beginning of our marriage, but I tried to get him there. I gave him books to read on spirituality, made him watch Oprah with me, and forced him to go here and there, thinking I had the answers for him. That experience taught me that you cannot pull someone on a different path or help them along if they're not ready. It becomes frustrating to you and them.

Back in 2004, I decided to go it alone, and the gap that already existed between us grew exponentially as I steered my own course, slowly and apprehensively. As the spiritual world opened up for me, I was further intrigued and wanted more of it. Every time I was doing what I liked, I felt satisfied, but every time I settled back into my life with Marlon, I came up empty. What I was seeking to free my soul did not exist within our union. The settling became unsettling.

Now, I was steering my own course unapologetically and gaining confidence. I might be fearful, even doubtful of the next step, but I was learning to trust.

With no more distractions, I was spending more time at home, which meant spending more time with Marlon. I yearned for so much more, but he was content with what we had. A quotidian relationship that was on a loop for over twenty years. I was seeing the full scope of our marriage, and with that came an intense loneliness. Nothing had improved since therapy. I had coped over the years with respites, but they were no longer sustaining me.

On September 4, 2010, I woke up feeling drained, sad, depressed, unhappy, unfulfilled, scared, and angry. I kept hearing, *More importantly, how can this last?* I grabbed a pencil and paper and started writing. What came out was a deep-seated truth I didn't want to admit. It came out in the form of a poem:

How Can This Last?
I'm your in-love moment,
you express every day.
And you're my moment of love
that has passed away.
I am your world
and you've made that known
I'm your life's dream you said,
but you're my moment in the sun.

You can live with part of me;
I can't live with all of you.
You're so easy to please,
But I'm insatiable.
You dwell in the shallow,
while I love to go deep,
Will you let me go now,
so I can breathe?

Will I break your heart
or set it free?
If you're standing still,
you can't see what I see.
How much more time

must continue to pass?
More importantly, how long can this last?

Tell me the meaning
of "til death do us part?"
'Cause I've died and reborn
several times from the start.
You don't realize,
you're still sleeping with the past.
More importantly, how long can this last?

I'd never written a poem before, and I was shocked when I was done. I gasped seeing my truth on paper.

My marriage was where I felt most stagnant, and I struggled to get through each day. My anxiety was returning, depression seemed closer than usual hovering over my head, and my sugar and caffeine addiction was on high again. What could I do to save this marriage? My husband did not want to do soul work and wanted to stay on the surface of things. I was embracing my soul work and going deeper. I loved and wanted personal growth and development. We were drifting further and further apart. Leaving seemed necessary. It was time to end my marriage. The consequences of my decision were going to break hearts, change lives, alter routines, and uproot folks, but I had to choose my soul. *I must choose me,* I reminded myself over and over.

The practice of choosing myself came through losing myself. Life experiences granted me opportunities for rediscovery. Every choice brought me closer or further away from who I am. I now choose the ones that bring me closer to my soul. Now, when negative emotions or a challenge arise, looking for ways to maintain my gainful ground becomes a priority—for I never want to lose me again. Eventually, ironing out the details of my modification won't feel like a daunting chore but an inspiring motive to stay on track with my soul's plan.

.   .   .

On September 17, Marlon and I had a sit-down about our marriage. I told him I wanted a divorce. "I'm not going to change my mind this time."

He said he would not agree to anything. I told him I was moving forward without him.

The last thing he said was, "I don't want a divorce, and I'm not telling the children."

I knew if I didn't inform our children, he would continue to ignore my request. I was afraid to do it all by myself. I didn't know how our children would react. It was difficult to get them all in one place given they were older now and had their own lives, so I jumped at the next availability. On September 24, I asked them all to the living room where Marlon sat on the couch watching television. I turned the television off and looked at Marlon. He folded his arms and shook his head no. I glared at him and raised my eyebrows. We were arguing without words when Kamilah said, "What's going on?"

I took my eyes off Marlon and said, "We're getting a divorce."

In that moment, I had just broken four hearts: the hearts of my three children and my spouse's heart. I just told the children we are splitting up. They were stunned, surprised, and in disbelief. The same feelings my husband had when I said I wanted a divorce over a decade ago. I felt nauseous and my stomach began to hurt. It was entirely my fault. I wanted this change, not my husband. Those were the saddest four faces I've ever seen. *What have I done?* I thought. The first hour was unbearable.

Our two daughters clung to each other and cried. Our son had a myriad of questions coming so fast that I was unable to keep up with him. Marlon said nothing. He answered nothing. I was in that familiar place in our marriage. I was driving the car of our marriage by myself. I was trying to respond to their questions, comments, and sadness as best as I could. I didn't want to damage them any further. I looked to Marlon several times for help but got no response. He just sat there looking sad and pitiful.

This was a critical turning point for our family. The beginning of the end to an epochal era. It was similar to when my parents, brothers, and I stepped off the plane in 1984; our lives were never the same. Life will never be the same for my current family either. But I won't repeat my parents' mistakes.

There was a lot for our children to understand, I know. But their poignant question was *why*? I told them the truth. "Your dad is the nicest guy in the world, and I love him, but I am not happy in this marriage, and I want to be happy."

None of them had been in a relationship to comprehend what I was talking about, so it was confusing for them. But I trusted that someday they would understand my point of view instead of me trying to convince them of it now.

Then Marlon finally spoke. "I don't want this divorce. Your mother does."

I didn't understand if he wanted to hurt me or make me look like the villain in front of the children. He had never done that before, so it took me by surprise.

"So, basically y'all been pretending this whole time? I hate fake shit. I'm leaving," Khaleel said, thumping down the stairs towards the front door.

"I just can't take this," Kamilah said, then grabbed her car keys and ran out the door behind Khaleel.

Kyra stayed in my arms and wept. Marlon left the room crying and stormed off to our bedroom. I stayed and cried with Kyra. Kyra eventually went to her own room, and I had to leave the house. I felt overwhelmed. I went to a nearby park and bawled.

I had taken a big step in my life. I knew it wasn't going to be easy for anyone. I hated to see my family distorted over my decision, but I had to continue the process of choosing me so as to not delay my journey. After a while, I felt relieved. The truth was out. I understood my son's anger about the pretending. Truth is always better than falseness. I took Kyra to get Italian ices so we could talk some more. Kamilah and Khaleel wouldn't take my calls.

"I want you to be happy, Mommy. I'm just sad that my parents are splitting up," said Kyra.

I called Kamilah several times, but she didn't answer. She answered when Kyra called her and said she was at her friend's house. "She needed to be away from us," Kyra told me.

Khaleel returned from the park shortly after Kyra and I arrived home. He spoke to his dad briefly, who was back in the living room watching television. I could hear Khaleel asking his father if he was okay, then he headed downstairs to his room. He didn't come talk to me. When Kamilah came home, she kissed her dad and asked him if he was okay. She stopped by my bedroom and said hi to me, then went to her room. I felt sad that neither she nor Khaleel asked me how I was doing. I felt I deserved to be ignored because I had created their sadness. But I know it was only for a brief period of time. Marlon didn't speak to me for the rest of the day and slept quite a distance away from me in bed that night. I expected his coldness. I felt very alone but relieved that the truth was on the outside of me and no longer posing as fear from within. At least for now, we were all on an authentic journey.

That was September 24, 2010, twenty-two years into our marriage. Our kids were twenty-one, fifteen, and twelve years of age. We lived the American dream in a suburban area of New Jersey, with a nice house and three cars. My husband made a good salary, and my children lived a seemingly charmed life. My spouse and I didn't fight, had a great sex life, were loving toward each other, and had built a loving home. But it wasn't enough. I'd been wanting a divorce for over a decade now and finally had the courage to take the necessary steps. I felt like a bird that always wanted to fly but didn't know it had wings.

We asked the children not to discuss the divorce with anyone, including extended family and their grandparents. I wanted this to be a private matter between us as a family without outside influence from anyone. I also didn't want anyone pitying my children and looking at them as if they were now flawed. They had enough adjustments to handle with this new epoch Mommy had ushered in for everyone. My children love both their parents very much, and we are a close-knit family. They grew up happy with parents who love them unconditionally. They were not marred; they were having to deal with a decision that was out of their control. I knew it would be hard on them, so Marlon and I agreed that he could stay in the house in a separate room until the divorce was final. I don't know if that was wise, but the kids were happy to have him there. We both wanted to be there for them as much as possible.

When I tried to engage Marlon about speaking to a lawyer, he said, "I'm not going to help you divorce me." So I chose to move forward alone. I had to be more courageous than I'd ever been in my life. Almost ten years ago, I wasn't brave enough to follow through with a divorce, but this time was different because I was different.

I had a consultation with a lawyer, attended classes at the courthouse, began filling out the forms, and had a consultation with a mediator. The first step is always the hardest, and I took it. I could feel Kadian with every step I took forward.

When Marlon saw what was happening, he began begging me to stop what I was doing. "Why are you doing this to me, to our children. I want you to stop it. Let's go back to therapy."

"We tried that already," I said.

"Okay, then I'll do what you want me to do. What do you want me to do?"

"I don't want you to change for me."

After a while, I stopped responding because his questions were becoming repetitive. As Marlon continued with his begging to help him understand why I was doing this to him and to our family, I could feel the space around us disappearing. I was now standing in a white room by myself when I heard my own unique tone say, *Because she's changed right before your eyes.* When I returned, Marlon was still quarreling.

Later that night, I revisited the day and what I had heard. And this poem came about:

You don't know what her favorite color is anymore,
Or the kinds of literature she adores
The conversations to ignite
Or the presents that excite
Because
She's changed
Right before your eyes.

You don't know what her dislikes are now
Or what are her new loves and new likes
So you guess and guess hoping to get it right
But you come up wrong,
Because
She's changed
Right before your eyes.

So, you delve into her world
Which makes your head turn,
You look at her in disbelief
and wondering why,
Because
She's changed
Right before your eyes.

The cocoon has opened
And out comes the butterfly,
She's lost to you now
And wondering where she's gone
Because
she's changed
Right before your eyes.

I was really getting acquainted with my tone and more in tune
with it. And mostly, I was paying attention. That poem was Kadian
speaking. I could feel her in the fibers of my being. Marlon hadn't

noticed how different I was. He thought he was still talking to Charm, that girl he'd met at eighteen and married at twenty-one. He couldn't see my growth or Kadian emerging. He wanted me to remain the same, locked up in a cocoon that was now much too small for me and feeling uncomfortable. It was stifling me. My breakthrough wasn't about him; it was for me. Our marriage was the cocoon encumbering my wings that were ready to spread.

Whenever I tried to discuss the divorce, Marlon ignored me. There were days he tried to make me feel guilty about what I wanted. He didn't understand that I wanted to feel passion outside the bedroom. I wanted fulfillment. I want authentic happiness to be my predominant nature instead of appearing for fleeting moments or in spurts. I wanted to experience things I'd never experienced before, like joy, intimacy, and purpose.

With each passing day since we told the kids, I felt less and less wishful and regretful about asking for the divorce. Two weeks before Thanksgiving, Ms. Brown called. I didn't answer the phone. I knew why she was calling. Then she rang Marlon. Ms. Brown wanted to know if we were coming for Thanksgiving. I told Marlon that I wasn't going to have the traditional Thanksgiving. "We're not visiting family and we're having a simple dinner at home." This upset him because I wouldn't partake in our traditional activities which perpetuate our marriage still being intact. I started to talk about moving forward with the divorce and wanted his opinion on some things such as lawyer vs. mediator or what to do about our home given Khaleel and Kyra were still teenagers. Marlon got quiet and unresponsive. After a while he finally spoke.

"I am begging you to stop moving forward." He was somewhat angry and sad at the same time.

I asked Marlon, "If I stop moving forward, what should I do about my happiness?" No response from him.

"Do you want me to go down that road of depression again?" Still no response.

"That's what will happen if I stay in this marriage. I would have to pretend that I am happy instead of experiencing real happiness."

My determinations weren't selfish. This was life and death for me. I would not survive another clinical depression. My parents' union gave me life, of course. I could imagine bursting into this world eager for what it had to offer for my soul to grow. But decisions were made for me without my input. Harmful things were said and done to me constantly. My life wasn't fed with proper nurturing, and it was difficult to evolve and grow within my situation. I lost the gleefulness from the beach and conformed and made do. My soul was stifled, and my life deteriorated as a result.

I wanted the life back into my heart and eyes. I wanted to live again and to live authentically. I was being pulled beyond my family's blueprint to follow my soul's intentions. Every choice is a possibility to achieve that. Choice is a tool to excavate and uncover our lost souls.

Ms. Brown called me a week before Christmas. This time I decided to answer the phone. I knew again why she was calling, and I wanted to be clear about my decision to not be in contact with her and the family. I could hear the hesitancy and fear in her voice before she asked if we were coming for the holiday or the New Year. Once again, I said no.

This time she asked, "Why?"

"I don't want to be in the company of people that do not serve my best interest whether they are friends or family. I need a break from you because the last three years have been difficult in your presence, and I'm taking this time to honor myself."

"Oh."

I wished her a happy holiday and hung up.

I told Marlon about the conversation with Ms. Brown. He did not look pleased but did not say anything about it. Instead, he asked me about my wedding ring and why I wasn't wearing it. I've had it off for two years now, and he hadn't had that request before.

"Putting on the ring isn't going to save our marriage," I said. "You know why."

"Well, I want you to put it on!" he yelled.

I knew he was still having a difficult time with this, but I was not putting it back on.

This had been an epic year of decision-making, and I had accomplished a great deal. I had bravely faced my past and the abuse. I had closed my last retail business, distanced myself from Ms. Brown, ended a dysfunctional friendship, and further delved into my spiritual growth. My depression had not entirely gone away from me. I knew exactly where it was. It was now locked in my inner confinements. I could sense its presence from time to time, but it was too weak to interrupt my life for now. The happier I got and the more I became dedicated to my soul's path, the more it cowered in fear. I'd found its kryptonite.

I hadn't been excited about a New Year coming in for a long time, but I was this year. I didn't make any New Year's resolutions. This time, I just wanted God to point me in the direction of my own personal happiness. This time was a different type of asking.

I stated aloud, "Show me happiness, God. Show it to me."

This would become my mantra for a long while. I wrote it often. I said it aloud. I whispered it. I said it in my mind. I cried it.

"Show me happiness, God. Show it to me."

CHAPTER TWELVE

The Year of Nurturing

I turned forty-four years old in January 2011, and I was living my life the most honest it had ever been. I was doing things that interested me and choosing me every step of the way. Marlon agreed to go to mediation with me after many discussions and arguments. The children now spoke more freely and easier about us divorcing. Kyra was more accepting than her siblings. She said nearly all her friends' parents were already divorced.

I was happy about the direction my life was moving in, especially with the possibility of a career change. I was thinking seriously about starting a Reiki practice as a new career, so I signed up to volunteer at a women's homeless shelter twice a month as a Reiki practitioner. I thought about this life change on the plane to Washington for my first mentorship class. My excitement about this new path soon turned to worry. Reiki was not a mainstream career. There isn't a degree to substantiate what I would be able to do energetically or psychically. This was different from starting up a retail store. For a moment, I was ecstatic, then ruminating on the details, I felt incompetent. *How can I do this*?

Each of my negative persuasions timestamped a possible future outcome I created with every thought. I could feel myself again as two contrasting entities. Where was the girl who was excited about this new change? And who was the girl who kept showing up sowing doubts?

I administered a Reiki self-treatment to calm my thoughts and my emotions. I closed my eyes and breathed. More hows about starting anew surfaced, but I kept breathing. I shifted my focus to my second chakra. I could feel energy swirling around between my physical body and my hand. I put my concentration there and soon felt my hand pulsating, then girdled with heat. My negative thoughts finally let go of me, and I relaxed in my seat.

Moments later, I heard: *Leave the hows alone. Concentrate on the now, not the how, for the now will answer all of your hows. It's time to trust the journey.*

Last year was the year of honesty for me. This year, I would nurture myself. Nurturing was not something I received growing up, therefore I am inclined to take care of myself last. It was time to change that. So, while in Washington this year, I would get acupuncture and acupuncture facials, massages, and energy healing, and I attended certain classes that I was interested in such as chakra clearing and mediumship. I completed my Reiki Master certification. I traveled to various islands in the Puget Sound of Washington and to the Gulf Islands in the Salish Sea to meet up with fellow safarians. I socialized with my classmates, had uplifting and encouraging talks, ate great food, and took long walks at Green Lake in Seattle.

I had a spectacular time on my trips. I've never spent that much time taking care of myself ever, and I loved every moment. I wished I had taken care of myself the way I took care of my children sooner.

Life at home was becoming frustrating as Marlon kept picking fights with me. The fights worsened the closer we got to our appointment date with the mediator.

Marlon kept insisting that he loved me. "I want you to stop this," he would say quite a lot.

I didn't doubt that Marlon loved me. He didn't understand that he hadn't grown in consciousness since I met him over twenty years earlier. It felt like he was stuck in the ebb of his life, and I'd finally found my flow. Now that the children were aware of our situation, they were no longer my anchor keeping me from drifting out to sea. I'd long since flowed away from his reach, but he still looked for me in the spot our wave crashed in on.

His capacity to love me seemed inadequate since I'd grown to love myself to a greater degree. His love now felt frigid instead of the warmth I once felt. And my new indicator to love myself wouldn't allow me to settle anymore. Marlon didn't understand that I had been feeling single for a while now. It just needed to be official. I hoped my leaving would awaken him to begin his journey to his own soul and find his flow.

During this time, Marlon was always emotional, and I understood his plight. Mostly anger stirred within him. He resorted to bargaining with me to keep our marriage together. "I'll turn the television off anytime you want me to or take it to the dump," he'd say.

His memory might have lapsed a bit, but mine had not. We had already gone through this in therapy. I saw him reading one of my spiritual books and wanting to discuss it with me.

"I'm trying to evolve. Give me a chance." That was his new word, "evolve." I'd given him over ten years to "evolve" and he hadn't tried. I told him again that I didn't want him to change for me. That kind of change is brief and futile, and also damaging to his own well-being.

I too was on an emotional rollercoaster. I was often alone in this divorce process as Marlon refused to help or comply with anything. I felt every emotion in existence—from sheer invigoration to the deepest sadness. Every single thing was coming up, including what I really meant, how I really felt, and what I really wanted—everything I hadn't said in the twenty-two years we were married. This purging left me drained, fearful, and full of doubts. More importantly, my whole being was yearning for change. If I did nothing, I was setting myself up for something more disastrous to happen. I ignored that doubtful girl and begged her to trust me.

Whenever I was in Washington, that doubtful girl would take a back seat because of the support system I had there. My mentoring classmates were my small community I could confide in when things became difficult. I was grateful for them during this challenging time in my life. I had surrounded myself with people who were understanding and respectful of my choices. In this space I could be my authentic self.

When I wanted to give up, this class and a few friends helped me to keep going. When I couldn't speak, words of encouragement were spoken until I found my voice again. When my energy was low, I made appointments with my mentor and summoned my classmates and friends to help me. When I couldn't get out of bed, I was encouraged to rest. We were all in a period of growth and helped each other along the way with the same goal in mind. We wanted to expand our light and be our authentic selves.

This mentoring environment helped me to go further within. I was entering that place where pieces of my soul were tethered. It made me stronger than ever. My marriage was a heavy, stagnant energy to dispel. I wasn't through it yet, but I could almost taste freedom and peace. The love for my children was my motivation for staying conscious in my life. But motivation is an external force that eventually diminishes, leaving me with no energy to keep going. I needed inspiration instead, that autonomous internal force. Inspiration came from my intense desire to know myself and pursue authentic happiness.

Finally, I was getting to know the real me. I was beginning to experience one of the most life-changing and extraordinary kinds of love there is—the love of self. With this love came a better understanding of who I was deep inside. Experiencing self-love expanded my capacity to love others and put me on a path of dedication to my soul.

The pain of splitting up my family was the hardest part for me and the biggest decision of my life, but I honored what I truly desired from the beginning—authentic happiness—so I stayed focused. Some days I couldn't get out of bed. Some nights I wanted to change my mind and go back to my husband, but whenever those feelings surfaced, I felt sicker and weaker. I couldn't stand settling anymore. Every time I considered settling again, other unsettling feelings rose up in me. I'd been down that road of pretending to be happy and trying to keep up with a life I no longer felt connected to, but I couldn't stay on that course any longer, not even for my children.

It was difficult being in the house with Marlon after a while. He swung from being angry to unresponsive. I looked for ways to keep myself centered and focused on the task at hand when I was back in New Jersey. I found a Buddhist temple near my home and went there on Saturday mornings to meditate.

One Saturday during the meditation, I found myself in a vision, surrounded by beautiful shrubs on either side of me. I looked ahead of me and saw Marlon standing quite a distance away. As he took steps towards me, the entrance to the path I was on closed in with shrubs. The closer he got to me, the smaller the entrance became until it was almost sealed off. I turned to an adjacent opening and walked towards it and out of the garden. Then I looked back and saw that the other opening was now closed off. I smiled as I turned around and began walking down this new path completely alone. Within a year of choosing me, my old path and old life seemed far away.

I was in close proximity to Kadian, and I could hear her voice more clearly each day. She beckoned me like my soul did. She was saying, *You are close to finding me. Don't give up now. Choose me, please.* And I did each time that year.

It was clear to me that the road to finding Kadian would be lonesome at first because everyone in my life then was standing on my old path that remained sealed and couldn't see the new one illuminated before me. They couldn't envision where I was headed and were unable to render the support necessary for me to venture forward. I trusted the new path would provide new relationships and experiences for me to find what I was searching for. I was starting over. Emptiness and disconnection from Kadian had overwhelmed me for most of my life. Kadian had been lost for far too long, and I desperately wanted to know her. I wanted to be her.

Marlon didn't know how to stop this train we were on. He flew to Florida to visit his parents to tell them about the divorce. He hadn't seen them in a while, and I thought a quick getaway would calm his emotions. Also, he needed people on his side to help him through this process as my classmates and my tiny group of friends did for me.

After Marlon came back from his trip, I elicited, sometimes demanded, honest conversations with him. He admitted he hadn't grown since we met but still wanted me to wait for him. I said, "I can't do that." He was more understanding this time. We were arguing less. The kids seemed their happy selves again, and I continued choosing me.

When summer approached, I called my oldest friend in North Carolina and told her what was happening in my life now. She was silent for a moment, then said, "Do you know when my husband and I want to get through a situation, we ask ourselves, 'What would Kadian and Marlon do?'" I wasn't surprised because I knew my marriage mirrored what people wanted. I just wished I was honest about it sooner. Even though she cared for Marlon, she said she supported me wholeheartedly.

Then I went to South Carolina to visit my other close friend. I needed space between me and Marlon, and I think he welcomed the space. My friend from South Carolina had known about the divorce for a couple of months now and although she loved Marlon, she supported me in my decision.

When I arrived home from South Carolina, I received a call from Ms. Brown. I don't know why I answered but I did. "Grandma had a stroke," she said.

The news devastated my family, especially Kamilah. My grandmother had her favorites among her grandchildren, and they knew who they were. Kamilah was one of them. We visited Grandma often in the hospital over the next few months. She had lost her mobility to walk and her ability to talk. She became depressed. Losing her independence overwhelmed her. At almost ninety years old, Grandma had always been able to physically take care of herself, and now she was disabled. Ms. Brown looked so worried. I wondered how she would cope given she'd been under Grandma's control her whole life. What would she do with herself? What impairment would she suffer without her mother's presence? Would she someday awaken to the captivity of her soul?

I could hear my younger cousins bickering as they approached Grandma's hospital room. My stomach was feeling queasy from not wanting to be in the same room with my biological family. Everyone pretending. Purposely behaving. Tensions building the longer we were in each other's presence. The normal rigmarole. I observed Ms. Brown inching closer to her family and further away from mine. Looking for acceptance from her mother as usual. Grandma would always have my mother's allegiance, and I would always feel alone in this company. This was my grandmother's legacy. A divided, pretentious group of beings, most gathered around her out of obligation instead of love.

I resumed calling Ms. Brown regularly to check on Grandma's progress, and she called to update me. All our conversations during this time were about Grandma. One night after leaving the hospital, I felt like I was standing in a flurry of rage. It came on unexpectedly. At first, I didn't know what was causing this volcanic eruption inside of me. Then I suddenly knew why. Spending time with Ms. Brown again triggered it. Having no contact with her all this time wasn't enough to move beyond our troubles. I sensed there was more soul work to be done.

After everyone went to bed, I sat down to do my guided visualization. I took the advice of my inner knowing to have a pad and pencil ready. I closed my eyes, took a deep breath, and allowed more shards of memory to come into view.

I see eight-year-old Charm sitting by Ms. Brown's bedside giving her a manicure and pedicure. This happens every weekend. If Ms. Brown has a function to attend and the nail color doesn't match her outfit, Charm has to change the nail polish color for that specific occasion. She has learned to do it neatly, else she gets slapped and told how sloppy she did Ms. Brown's nails, and then she has to re-polish them. Ms. Brown doesn't feel she should get things professionally done. That is why Charm is there. Ms. Brown doesn't want a daughter; she wants an indentured servant.

I look deeper into this memory and see family coming over every weekend. No matter what Charm is doing with her cousins, she has to stop to clean the kitchen, or do Ms. Brown's nails, or whatever is asked of her. She hardly ever gets to just play like everyone else. My cousins are jeering me because I always have chores to do. Ms. Brown doesn't care that they mock Charm; and that only encourages the shaming. I find the source of my queasiness. When my cousins are around, I tense up, waiting for Ms. Brown to shame me.

I felt a deeper level of anger rising to the surface to be acknowledged and caressed by me. It was front and center, waiting to explode. I grabbed the pad and pencil and wrote:

> *Charm, you're so fucking stupid. You freckled-face girl. You bow-legged, red-face girl like your father.*

I felt my soul fragmenting and being encapsulated each time Ms. Brown said those words to me. I continued writing. When I was done, I had put twelve thousand words of pain to paper. I felt tremendous relief after writing those words as the pain from my past flowed from my body onto the piece of paper, making me feel somewhat lighter.

I woke up angry the next morning, needing to get going on my day because I had a few things to do, but I couldn't move. My anger confined me to my bed. I laid there with my past reverberating in my head while memories of that powerless little girl floated by with each intense, rapid rise and fall of my chest. *How can I let go of this dysfunctional and strained relationship with Ms. Brown?* It was as if all my wondering was posing a question I needed to answer at that moment.

Finally, the intensity of my breath subsided as silence intruded upon my thoughts. I could hear my unique tone buzzing in my left ear and encircling my being. Soon after, a sense of peace and relief came over me. The world went dark, and I found myself in that infinite space again.

I don't know how long I lingered there when a visual appeared:

I see a plentitude of pregnant women everywhere. They have one thing in common: they're about to give birth. Looking closer, I see almost invisible, clear tubes attached to the belly button of each woman. The tubes, like everything else, are energy. Following the energy tubes with my eyes, looking up at what seems like miles out into space, something is coming into view as planet Earth is fading. I notice I am above Earth out in the cosmos somewhere. The tubes are attached to a type of apparatus suspended in the air. The apparatus looks like an airplane without its wings but with translucent tubes coming from it. The elongated tubes are everywhere—hundreds, thousands, hundreds of thousands, perhaps millions of them— hovering over Earth. Observing more closely, I can see souls diving into the tubes to move towards their incarnation. I am in awe of what is happening.

I am taken to a specific apparatus. A closer view reveals that the apparatus is not shaped like an airplane but is shaped more like a dome. Picture a jellyfish with an opaque head and translucent legs. There's no color to the apparatus, and it is moving slowly the way a jellyfish will move in the water. I can identify most of the souls on the specific apparatus in my view. I recognize my great-grandparents, grandparents, parents, brothers, sisters, friends, almost-ex-spouse, my children, teachers, and many relationships I have encountered in this life. They are not in physical form, but I am able to identify them by their individual energy. There were souls I didn't recognize (maybe souls I haven't met yet or our paths haven't crossed due to the choices I or they have made). Each soul is filled with glee awaiting its turn to incarnate onto the earth's school.

Right before one soul jumps into its tube, an exchange of words between the jumper and the awaiting souls happens. The next exchange appears before me. This exchange is between Ms. Brown and me. Before she jumps, she looks at me, soul to soul with tremendous love, and speaks. "During the course of this lifetime together on Earth, I may lose connection with my soul. As a result, I may cause you pain. Please forgive me! Remember, whatever I think, say, or do, the underlying message is always love. Thank you for taking this journey with me and the opportunity to advance my soul's evolution."

I respond to my Ms. Brown, saying, "Thank you for taking this journey with me and the opportunity to advance my soul's evolution. Most importantly, thank you for reminding me of my greatness."

While jumping into her tube, she gestures one last time, this time to all the souls on the apparatus, "Thank you and I love you all," and she moves towards her birth canal. Somehow, I know that this exchange is done between every individual soul before each incarnation.

My vision fast-forwarded to my exchange with my children.

Before I jump, I look at them individually, soul to soul with tremendous love, and say, "During the course of this lifetime together on Earth, I may lose connection with my soul. As a result, I may not be the best I can be and may cause you pain. Please forgive me! Remember, whatever I think, say, or do, the underlying message is always love. Thank you for taking this journey with me and the opportunity to advance my soul's evolution."

They respond collectively, "Thank you for taking this journey with us and the opportunity to advance our soul's evolution. Most importantly, thank you for reminding us of our greatness."

An enormous energy of love and compassion envelops me. This energy permeates my soul as all the souls utter in unison, "During the course of this lifetime on Earth, you may lose connection from your soul. As a result, you may mistreat us and yourself, causing yourself tremendous pain. Please forgive yourself!"

Falling towards my tube, I gesture one last time to everyone. "Thank you and I love you all."

This visualization became a tool to help me practice forgiving my mother. I concentrated especially on the love and compassion I received from the other souls and their advice: "Please forgive yourself!" This has helped me in many ways, since I too have caused pain in others due to my words or actions. I see it as a lesson not just in love and compassion but also in understanding and empathy.

Obligatory relationships are inauthentic, and they are not love. My guided visualizations helped me become confident in my conviction to not partake in obligatory relationships regardless of who the person is. Continuing the visualizations was a huge undertaking and not a popular exercise one would choose to do— especially with a parent—but our soul doesn't abide by our earthly rules or dynamics. And as my own personal level of consciousness grew, I doubled down in my conviction.

I wondered if Ms. Brown would one day choose to change familial patterns. Would she come on this journey of love with me so we could finally be mom and daughter? Only time will tell. When I was about four years old, I heard Mama say, "You don't have to fight battles. Time will fight for you. Time is the greatest weapon on earth." I didn't understand what that meant until later in life. You will not always be trapped where you are. Time helps you see certain things, people, and everything around you with a new perspective, even hurt and betrayal. Time is the greatest weapon on earth because it heals wounds and brings understanding to situations previously hard to comprehend.

There's nothing that can be destroyed that time can't bring back anew.

I may not have an earthly mother in my corner, but I felt free. Free to pursue unobligated relations with her and free to live authentically. I no longer lived on the outskirts of two different realities with no connection to my internal home for guidance.

In late August, I called Ms. Brown to tell her about the divorce. She was quiet for a moment, then said, "If you're not happy, then you should proceed." I was a little surprised by her response given her previous outlook about changing my life. I didn't respond immediately. Then she said, "I will always love Marlon, and he will always be my son. Did the kids know when they visited me in July?"

"Yes, we told them last September."

There was a pause. "Wow. They spent five days with me in July, and there was no hint from them about what was going on. They seemed so happy."

I explained that Marlon and I did not want any interference from anyone during this process, so we asked them not to.

Afterwards, I called my father and told him about the divorce. "What did he do?" he asked.

"Nothing," I said.

"Charm, did he cheat?"

"No, Dad. If only it was that easy for me to leave."

"I don't understand leaving because you're not happy. No one divorces because they're not happy. My daughter, be honest with me, what did he do?"

I don't know if I ever convinced my father that unhappiness is a real reason for divorcing.

It was a gorgeous day outside on September 9. I sat in my car under my favorite tree and felt amazing for no particular reason. The different colors and shapes of the leaves, the variety of trees, the roses across the street, the different sizes, shapes, and colors of the cars that were in motion, and the different individuals out and about. Even in the red drink held by that lady coming out of Starbucks. I wondered what it was called because it looked refreshing. I felt so in tune. I felt another poem coming on and started writing.

When I was done, I had penned lines to a new poem, "Afraid to be Seen."

> Afraid of my own light,
> So I hid,
> Couldn't face my own greatness,
> So I blended in,
> Didn't see my own beauty,
> So I hid,
> Couldn't stand to be different,
> So I did what they did.
> They were afraid of my light,
> So I hid,
> They couldn't face my greatness,
> So I blended in,
> They didn't see my beauty,
> So I hid,
> They wanted me to be different,
> So I did.
>
> Afraid to be seen,
> So I hid,
> Escaping vulnerability
> Is how I hid.
> I covered myself
> And twisted the lid.
> Not letting you in
> Was how I lived.
>
> Then one day the Universe

Shouted my name,
Explained my own light,
Beauty and grace.
No longer afraid
To be seen or fit in,
I accepted love
And untwisted the lid.

Embracing vulnerability
Is now my bid.
I acknowledged my greatness
And no longer hid.

I sat there looking at my words when I heard: *I am here to remind you of your greatness.*

Those words permeated my being like shock waves, and things became pristinely clear in that moment. Charm, my inner protagonist, was a pretender. She wanted nothing to disrupt the life she had settled into. She was the conformist me. The aggressive me. The pretend me. Charm wasn't going to eradicate patterns, look for her greatness, or transform her life if left alone. That's who Marlon loved. The small me. Kadian, my inner antagonist, represented my truth. She loved change. She loved to disrupt. She was Charm's greater potential. She was the one Marlon couldn't keep up with. She was the one he wanted to stay silent.

Whenever I landed at Newark Airport, coming back from Seattle, I wished I was visiting instead of coming home. My home inside was different. This life was beginning to feel old. It felt as if I had one foot in the past and the other in the present, and I was wavering back and forth.

I went to the courthouse on November 2 to file for divorce and received our court date, December 15. It was three days before

Kamilah's birthday. I'm so glad it didn't fall on her day. I told
Marlon about the divorce date when he arrived home from work.

He said, "I won't go to the courthouse with you."

I expected that would be what he would say.

"I'll begin looking for a place to live on the weekend." It was
the last thing he said to me for the rest of the night and for a few
days afterwards.

The children and I visited Grandma in the hospital often. By
November, she looked so despondent. I could tell she didn't want
to be here any longer. I wondered if she wanted permission to
leave. It would make a lot of us sad, including me, but I wanted
her to do what she wanted, not what we wanted for her.

My mother asked if we could please come for Christmas
dinner. She would be having a family get-together for Grandma.
She was not sure how much longer Grandma would have here on
earth. I said we would be there.

A few days before Christmas, I went to lunch one afternoon
with a friend. After telling her about my divorce, she confessed
that she had been secretly jealous of my growth for a while and
especially now that I had the courage to divorce Marlon. She'd
been wanting to divorce her husband but didn't have the courage
to do it. I'd known this lady for over twenty years, and she'd always
been into spiritual ideology. When she first tried to introduce spiritual ideas to me, I couldn't comprehend what she was talking
about because they were out of my purview, and so I ignored her.
Now she was jealous of my growth.

Sometimes one can seem aware and awake but have very little
growth. Someone could awaken in a given moment and have
tremendous growth, and it may seem to others as if this happened
in the blink of an eye. But it did not. It's the many beckonings from
the soul. It's following through with the hard decisions afraid and
without support. It's being unafraid to walk on the road less traveled. A zest and thirst for happiness and soul expansion are all that

are required to dedicate oneself. Nothing will come between us and who we are supposed to be, even when everyone else thinks we are crazy or wrong.

I was awakened by a soft, piercing sound protruding from my ear on the morning of December 15, 2011. I laid still, soaking in its caress, with my eyes still shut. The sound traveled around my head and filled my body. Without amplifying, it unfurled onto my room, house, and forty-four-year existence. It was my unique tone with a new intent I didn't recognize at first because it had never expanded beyond my physical body. It wasn't escorted by a message either. Just an overwhelming feeling of happiness that hadn't been constant in my life. It felt almost blissful and somewhat familiar. It was the breeze traveling through my fingers and plaits. The smell of the saltwater as I approached the beach as a child, the astounding beauty of the horizon. I wondered what was causing this felicitous feeling. Then it dawned on me; it was the day of my divorce. Not ours, but mine.

I turned on my left side and opened my eyes to find a note and a red rose from Marlon staring me in the face.

> *Don't do this. I'm begging you. I'll do anything, just give me another chance.*

I tore the note into pieces.

I heard my phone beeping. There were several text messages from him, pleading with me not to go to the courthouse. Today would be the last day of our twenty-two-year marriage, and this was his last-ditch hope of changing my mind. Nothing was going to ruin this feeling or turning point for me. I ignored them all and got out of bed, got dressed, and got divorced.

CHAPTER THIRTEEN

Leaving a Legacy

On January 4, 2012, I was sitting on the edge of the bed after a shower when a surge of energy passed through my body. I immediately fell ill. I ran to the bathroom to throw up. I went back to my bedroom and doubled up in pain, then the pain went away the way it came, suddenly.

My phone rang and it was Ms. Brown, "Your grandmother passed a few minutes ago."

"I know."

"How do you know?"

"I felt her."

My grandmother was the end to a generation on my maternal side. Another generation gone and leaving a mess for the rest of us to clean up. There was a time when I couldn't breathe from inhaling the pile of karmic dust contaminating my life that previous generations had left behind. But these last few years of purifying my own personal air space had enabled me to begin breathing in clean air again.

Whenever a generation dies off, it bequeaths scores of unhappy, depressed beings who become lost in this world. Beings whose souls will have to work hard at reconnecting with their human self. Eradicating patterns, dismantling outdated beliefs, and being honest about the people who birthed us will begin that process of cleaning up their messes to forge authentic, loving relationships with future generations.

Grandma's death brought forth the usual rigmarole of arguments and even more ugliness than usual amongst family members; also, some honest truths that needed to be said. Ms. Brown, of course, wished I hadn't said anything and wanted to let things slide. She only wanted to complain in private to me. Ms. Brown did what she always does: complained to me, then smiled in her family's faces, and when I addressed issues, she became unhappy with me.

Most family members were distraught at the funeral as guilt washed over them. There was the guilt of not spending time with Grandma and helping her even though they lived within a few miles of her. Regrets spilled from their energy, especially the ones she adored. My children and I were guilt-free. We spent more time with Grandma than everyone (except Ms. Brown) even though we lived sixty miles away. Grandma and I had our share of honest conversations and disagreements. I sensed her soul desperately wanting to break through during those vulnerable moments together. If only we had started the journey to our souls together sooner. I might have been the only person to go as deep as I did with her.

After Grandma's funeral, Ms. Brown began calling me more. I chose to answer when I wanted to, but not out of obligation or fear. I believe she thought that our relationship was the best it had ever been. And she was correct, compared to how it was before Grandma's passing. But I knew the storm had only calmed down for now because most of her time was occupied still processing her mother's death. She began clinging to her family more than ever, and I chose not to interact with most of them when I drove away from the cemetery. Where my relationship with Ms. Brown was headed seemed up in the air for now.

Likewise, after Brian's funeral, my father and I had begun to develop a relationship. I was hoping to have something greater with him, but it was not possible. To develop a closeness with my father meant I'd have to operate on his terms in his reality. This meant I had to become Adrian's caregiver and financially assist him in his struggle to live in this world. I was not going to take up that role again. I only had three children. So, we became estranged again for a time.

Adrian continued to struggle, and I needed to separate myself from his situation altogether. I did not accept calls or visit him in Jamaica. For the first time in my life, I felt free of tremendous obligation to him. I want to stay focused on my path. There was a greater Kadian up ahead waiting for me.

I have observed five generations of harm in my maternal family. I want to leave my children with a different type of legacy. I want to bequeath them a new family tree by breaking off my branch. Planting it in an undisclosed location and watering it differently from my family of origin. I'm not going to water it with obligation and the challenges that come with that. But with love, compassion, freedom to express, and allowing them to be who they are in this world. The way Mama tried with my brothers and me. I want to teach my children not to open their future-generation pods too soon, but to preserve and protect their innocence as long as possible. Let them feel safe and empowered. Then, when their own ackee pods open naturally, they can contribute to the world the humanity it needs.

Most importantly, I'll continue to eradicate the patterns I've inherited—and the self-created ones—and teach my children to do the same. This will allow them to start on their soul's expansion sooner, not having to work tediously through previous generational patterns and outdated beliefs. This is more important than gifting them money or property.

Why focus on leaving generational wealth when your loved

ones are stuck in generational traumas? What is the use of money
and property if your loved ones are miserable?

I have released tremendous pain from my childhood. I know
my emotional release is not over, but I have gained some ground. I
have tackled the eradication of the mother-daughter dysfunctional
patterns on Ms. Brown's family branch that kept me small. And I
will break that branch off soon enough to begin tending to my own
family tree. To be my own gardener and cultivate my grounds the
way I want.

I can now trust myself not to be rageful towards my mother as
she gets older. I can be kind to her, and my kindness will be
coming from an authentic place. I have no wishes about our relationship. I am going to allow my soul to continue to guide me. My
life is now about the choices I'll make when life feels uncomfortable.

Marlon attended Grandma's funeral and accepted the call to be one
of the pallbearers. Family members were informed of our divorce
by then. The disbelief, perplexed looks, and lack of understanding
validated not telling them sooner. It seemed some of them needed
therapy for my divorce. Marlon moved out and was angrier than
ever. He refused to discuss anything with me, whether it was about
the children, our house, or anything else. Only time will tell what
our relationship will become. Time is the greatest weapon on
earth.

My children adjusted to their new life. The last few months of
2012 had been hard for them. They'd lost their great-grandmother,
and for the first time in their lives, their father was not in the same
home with them. Our new reality wasn't going to be easy because
several factors were involved. First, they were all young adults
looking to follow their own course, and I knew more than anyone
else what that process entailed. It wouldn't be an easy road if my
children choose to take on generational patterns or any patterns.
They weren't exempt from what the past generation left behind or

from whatever patterns had formed between them and their parents and each other. Second, I planned to be honest with them. I didn't always get it right, but I was willing to continue on my journey of authentic happiness and to be a light for them to observe. I promised to choose me no matter what. My children wouldn't agree with all of my choices, but we were starting from a better place than the previous generation. I was a different mother, and some of the patterns did not affect them as much. They had less fumigating to do.

I awakened on Thanksgiving Day to a quiet, still house. The children were with Marlon for the holiday. As I stood in my kitchen stirring my morning tea, I felt nothing, nothing at all. It wasn't emptiness or sadness. But this nothingness had no weight attached to it. I could no longer sense the shroud I had come to live with for nearly two decades. I closed my eyes and continued stirring. Where was my depression? I stood in my kitchen feeling unperplexed, unfearing, and unburdened.

I left my tea on the counter and opted for a walk instead to look deeper within. I searched about for my depression and found nothing. Not even the chamber where I held it. I could only imagine it slowly starving while I kept choosing myself—and finally both depression and its chamber gradually disintegrated. And through the window of my life, a breeze came and blew the remaining particles into the ethers. Depression was no longer mine, and I was truly alone in peaceful solitude.

I began walking briskly. I launched into a jog, then took off running. It had been years since I'd run, having been overweight for a while now. I wanted to jump up and down and do cartwheels. I didn't know where this energy was coming from. And when I stopped running, I had logged over a mile. My epoch of depression had ended, and an empowered era had begun for me. I wasn't entirely free of concerns or all fears, for I sensed the fears associated with the new paths up ahead. But this time I would go into my future unappendaged. There was nothing left to manage anymore, and I had no fear of this megrim returning. It was

entirely gone. I had done it without medication and lifelong therapy. I knew I had beaten the odds in an age when most are bound
to this ugly enemy.

Authentic happiness isn't a specific moment but rather an
accumulation of genuine moments. The process of undoing your
modification will create more genuine moments. This is soul work.
When life is no longer determined by the restrictions placed on
you by society, family, or friends, then you can honestly say your
soul is free. My soul is preparing to take flight.

As I started to evolve, so did my story. I had focused so much
on what was wrong in my life and with my parents and other relationships that I didn't remember experiences of authentic happiness. When I began to unload the residue of my emotional
traumas, I was able to retrieve many happy childhood memories.

CHAPTER FOURTEEN

Rewriting My Story

My story begins with my birth on the beautiful island of Jamaica in the capital of Kingston. At age six, I was afforded an opportunity that many people will never get: I arrived in the United States of America, a legal resident. I am grateful to my parents for giving me that opportunity, something they themselves had to work hard to achieve.

Love comes in different forms and degrees. My parents loved me enough to want a better life for me. When I landed here, those two brave souls knew I was destined for something greater than what they could imagine. They knew it in the deepest part of their core and wanted to help me achieve that. Their methods and ideals were different, but the underlying goal was to get me where I needed to go.

During our first winter in America, my brothers and I stood in amazement at how cold it got, and we experienced a snowfall, unaware that this thing existed. We learned to ride sleds and had fun practicing on the steep hill on our block. My brothers and I weren't used to the snow or cold, so every hour we would run upstairs to keep warm. Ms. Brown had hot chocolate with marsh-mallows in it and graham crackers waiting. It was so delicious. Then we would run back downstairs after we weren't cold anymore to play in the snow again. We did this over and over. As I am writing this, I feel so much joy inside because that was truly a fun and happy time. It was one of the rare occasions I wasn't in trouble and was allowed to simply be a child and play.

My parents sent us to Jamaica during summer holidays, and we stayed the whole summer. While we were climbing Dunn's River Falls or soaking in one of the island's hot springs such as Milk River Bath or swimming in the many natural rivers, most of the children in our neighborhood of the Bronx never ventured far from the block of Ogden Avenue. Our friends either visited the local pool where they had to wait in line for hours to get in or they turned on the hydrants to keep cool on a humid day.

When I was seventeen, my father granted me the opportunity to begin my soul's journey by pushing me out into the world early. He did not possess the consciousness, awareness, or capacity to guide me. And in a moment of frustration, he unconsciously set me free. His soul knew the Universe had me under Its wings.

When I separated myself from Ms. Brown as a result of her actions in our relationship, she unconsciously came to the same conclusion my father did earlier. She did not possess the consciousness, awareness, or capacity. She herself was bound in generational dynamics and therefore couldn't assist me with what I needed. She unconsciously gave me the space to walk away. In the deepest part of her soul, she knew the Universe would protect, guide, and keep me safe on my own individual journey.

Although I left my mother's home, I still played in that reality of old patterning because I kept those same negative stories with me and told them often to myself, which conjured up past emotions and traumas. They would control my life for years. I have changed some patterns between Ms. Brown and me. Her mother died without her changing the patterns that existed between them. My mother's relationship with me may never be ideal, but at least I changed that parent-child relationship pattern that I saw playing out in my family.

How brave they were to take on this assignment as my parents before they entered the earth plane, knowing that someday they might be talked and written about so publicly. As my parents took on this assignment with love from their souls, they wanted to partake as best as they could in helping me align to greater versions of myself. That's soul love, not earthly love.

My life changed when my father threw me out, but I kept the old life with me because I dwelled only on the negative aspects of that reality. My past was traveling with me each time I ventured down new paths. It was never far behind, but writing has helped me put some distance between me and my past. Now when I remember the unpleasant times, I am equipped with the tools to bring them up and out of my energy system instead of allowing them to continue to fester. Forgiveness is a continual process. It will take some time to forgive my parents.

In college, I met my future husband, Marlon. He happened to be from my homeland of Jamaica. The Universe knew I needed love, peace, and stability in my life and provided that for me in Marlon. This man loved me to the best of his ability, and it was evident to him as well that my destiny was to find my greatness path. This man provided me the environment to explore, knowing that one day I might embark upon that journey without him because he too did not possess the consciousness, awareness, and capacity to walk it with me. He himself was not seeking his soul and couldn't assist me the way I needed to be assisted. So, he did what he knew to do: he let me go. In the deepest part of his soul, he knew the Universe would provide for me what was limited in him, and he knew I'd be just fine.

As I approached John F. Kennedy Airport in October 1973, enjoying my first airplane ride and seeing those tall buildings lit up from the sky, I knew my life would never be the same. And it never was. America was now my home and a place where great things would emerge for me and from me. America is abundant in opportunities, rich in experiences, grounded in creativity, paved with possibilities, progressive in ideas, and filled with choices. Jamaica grounded me and made me strong and brave to take on the quest of my soul, while America fed my mind, emptied my thoughts, released my obligations, and freed my soul. America was where I was able to challenge my mother, break patterns, and become brave enough to leave a marriage. America became the heart of my journey and where I rediscovered authentic happiness.

Being set free, pushed out, and let go of led me to paths hidden away by karmic dust. As I stand before these paths in anticipation but with a bit of hesitation, a realization sets in. My life was never about blending into a culture or society; it wasn't just to aspire or inspire, but to embrace my individualization. We are here to connect to our light, not to conform; to walk in it, not to blend in; to expand it and not to diminish it. When we conform and blend in, we diminish our own light, and the world becomes a dark room where the blind lead the blind.

As I continue my spiritual development, my story continues to unfold and expand. As I continue on my journey to my greatness, my story is always evolving and magical. This is my new story. This is my own song.

Acknowledgments

Kamilah, Khaleel, and Kyra, thank you for all you do in helping Mommy expand her light. I admire your outspokenness, truths, strengths, courage, and souls. Thank you for agreeing to rendezvous with me in this life as we help each other on our way to our greatness.

In loving memory of my brother, Brian Brown, who never felt authentic happiness or got to know his authentic self before he left this planet. Thinking of you many times during this book has inspired me to continue finding deeper levels of happiness in my life. I couldn't save you or change your reality, yet I know you are with me every step of the way on my journey. I love you. Until we meet again...

To my brother, Adrian Brown (Brian's twin), who has decided to remain here on planet Earth to continue his soul work. I admire your strength, courage, and attempts at happiness and peace. Don't give up yet; your soul is still trying to connect. I love you.

Ms. Brown, Mom, we chose to rendezvous together in this life and it hasn't been easy for either of us. But thank you for being part of my journey to finding Kadian and authentic happiness again. You didn't do it through wise words, or being a great mother, or kindness but you did it the only way you knew how—through contrast. That works too.

Shelly Francis, the cliché "There are no words to describe..." applies here. You understood my vision for my book from the beginning. Thank you for bringing that vision to fruition, but most importantly, I'm grateful for your mentorship, professionalism, patience, and understanding. You were the wind beneath my wings. I couldn't have done it without you.

Megan Reynolds, when I was asked if we were "best friends," I couldn't respond right away because it didn't feel right or appropriate. Later we found what fit better. So, my sister, thank you for the encouragements, your time and space, and the words you spoke to me to help me believe in myself and move this book forward: "I will invest in you."

Thank you, Genie Reynolds, for loving your daughter the way you do. Your love shows up in many ways, especially in the way you believe and trust her judgments. Thank you for helping me bring this book to life because of that trust.

I'm grateful, Kristen Peters, for the time you took out of your life to be an early reader. Your honest feedback brought about a significant change in the timeline and clarity that my book needed.

Thank you, Fiona Sturrock, for being one of my early readers. I really appreciated your constructive feedback and support.

Special acknowledgments to Keith Shepherd for your beautiful artwork and vision. Thank you, Anthony Simpson, for your relentless efforts to find the perfect ackee to photograph for the cover. And thanks to Claude Pierre-Val for your digital finessing.

To the many souls who have helped this book come about through our encounters and life experiences, thank you from the deepest part of my soul for being a part of my journey.

About the Author

Kadian Grant uses her intuitive talents and real-life experiences to facilitate the growth and development of souls. As an author and pattern-eradicator, she loves to inspire individuals in their spiritual and emotional healing. Kadian graduated from Cheyney University of Pennsylvania and is a Distinguished Toastmaster. She is a certified Stretch practitioner and Reiki master. Kadian lives in Piscataway, New Jersey, close to her three amazing adult children and one adorable granddog. Join her online at KadianGrant.com, at Facebook.com/kadianrg, and on Instagram at @askkadian where she'll be "reminding you of your greatness!"

Kadian is available to speak to book clubs online or in person.

**CREATIVE
COURAGE
PRESS**

Creative Courage Press is a small, independent publishing company founded in 2020 by Shelly L. Francis, inspired by the people she met while writing *The Courage Way: Leading and Living with Integrity*. Now, in collaboration with other authors, we are creating courage for the complexity of being human.

Get to know the essential voices of our remarkable authors and their refreshing ideas for leading change from the heart. Together we hope to generate meaningful conversations in our communities.

Visit us online to get fortified with resources and reflections for creating your own courageous way of life. As we grow, we invite you to grow with us.

www.CreativeCouragePress.com
hello@CreativeCouragePress.com

www.ingramcontent.com/pod-product-compliance
Lightning Source LLC
Chambersburg PA
CBHW031511120626
46545CB00005B/1834